KINGDOM
BEYOND BORDERS

· · · · · · · · · · · · · · · · · · · ·

Finding Hope Along the Refugee Highway

Helena Smrcek

WestBow
PRESS
A DIVISION OF THOMAS NELSON

WestBow Press books may be ordered through booksellers or by contacting:

WestBow Press
A Division of Thomas Nelson
1663 Liberty Drive
Bloomington, IN 47403
www.westbowpress.com
1-(866) 928-1240

ISBN: 978-1-4497-1566-3 (sc)
ISBN: 978-1-4497-1567-0 (e)

Library of Congress Control Number: 2011926878

Printed in the United States of America

WestBow Press rev. date: 10/12/2011

It has been my privilege to know Scott and Vicki McCracken for over 25 years. Their passion and love for refugees, the disenfranchised and the marginalized has been unwavering. One of the great themes of the Biblical narrative is God's love for the alien and how people of faith should demonstrate hospitality. It is my hope and prayer as you read these daily devotionals that your concern for modern day aliens –refugees– will go deeper and wider, reflecting God's heart of grace and love.

Dr. Geoff Tunnicliffe
CEO/Secretary General
World Evangelical Alliance

The profound ministry of International Teams among refugees in Athens is meeting desperate men, women and children with compassionate help and life-giving hope in the name of Jesus. How like our God to meet people in their darkest moment! Let the true stories in this book be an inspiration as you rediscover the truth that the apostle Paul once proclaimed in the Areopagus; "...[God] *determined the times set for them and the exact places where they should live. God did this so that men would seek him and perhaps reach out for him and find him...*" Acts 17:26, 27

Tom Albinson
President
International Association for Refugees

These stories of refugees caught in the crossfire of cultural, political and religious turmoil will touch your heart. The Holy Spirit guided and directed them toward the light of God's power and salvation, and their stories will thrill your heart and challenge you to action.

Kevin G. Dyer PhD
Founder International Teams

Just as Jesus revealed profound truth through human stories, Kingdom Beyond Borders reveals the profound impact of ministry to the souls-without-hope who travel the Refugee Highway. The stories told in this book will leave you shaking your head at the pain and loss experienced by so many...and leave you celebrating the transformational power of the Gospel to bring them lasting hope.

Craig Glass
President, Peregrine Ministries

These are the true stories of refugees in our time! Suffering, fear and brutality are met and overcome by hope, love and forgiveness. If you have any interest in what God is doing in our world, this is a book for you!

Neil Ostrander
CEO, International Teams Canada

Abraham, Moses, David, Israel and Jesus were all refugees which makes this book a lot like the Bible. You will celebrate these stories of life change among refugees and those who serve them. This book will expose you to a large and largely overlooked people group, many of whom are finding their way to Jesus. Read this book with an open heart and encounter afresh the God who never gives up on lost and wondering humanity.

Don Golden
Senior Vice President of Church Engagement at World Relief

My eyes welled up with tears as I read the opening chapters of this captivating book. I was struck by the honest representation of lives so different from my own. The compelling storytelling, and clear connection with the hope we have in Christ deeply moved me. I am so grateful for missionaries like Scott and Vicki McCracken who are the hands and voice of Jesus to those who desperately need His touch. Anyone who touches these pages will be touched with the reality of our needy world and the practical and eternal provision of our kind Father. This was totally inspiring!

Jennifer Rothschild
Author of *Lessons I Learned in the Dark and Self Talk, Soul Talk: What to Say When You Talk to Yourself*
Founder of www.womensministry.net

I have known my dear friends, Scott and Vicki McCracken, more than 25 years. Their love for God and people has deepened throughout the years in their ministry to refugees. Out of all the books you read this year, none will grip your heart more than 'Kingdom Beyond Borders'.

Frank Ley
Community Pastor
Willow Creek Community Church
S. Barrington, IL.

For more than two decades, Scott and Vicki McCracken have been sending letters every few months with stories exactly like those found in the riveting chapters of this book—refugees who find themselves against all odds, escaping desperate situations and finding themselves in Athens, Greece, with little or nothing but the clothes on their back. Through the caring ministry of Helping Hands that provides practical help for refugees' physical needs, and through the love exuding from lives transformed by Jesus Christ, refugee after refugee from whatever background-Muslim, Communist, atheist, comes to follow Jesus. Dreams, visions and miracles directly from Christ make these true stories that much more stunning. A must read for anyone whose faith ever needs encouragement, or wonders if true, holistic Christianity exists anywhere in the world. Praise God for this phenomenal ministry!

Craig L. Blomberg
Distinguished Professor of New Testament
Denver Seminary, Littleton, Colorado, USA

Table of Contents

Foreword

In the summer of 1984 God touched my heart concerning overseas missions. After years of intentionally avoiding Keith Green's tract, "Why You Should Go to the Mission Field," I finally broke down and read it the summer after I graduated from Palm Beach Atlantic College. I gave in because I had already made a commitment to work in the fall as a live-in counselor at a Christian drug rehab program (the Teen Challenge Center of Wheeling, West Virginia).

I was immediately on my face after reading the tract, weeping before God, and telling Him that, if He wanted me to go, I was willing. I went to work at Teen Challenge with missions on the back burner of my mind. I read books and magazines about missions and applied to a few organizations. International Teams accepted me for their new ministry to refugees in Austria.

The next catalytic, life-changing year for me was 1986. It was in this year I started the seven month training program with International Teams, which was the place where I met and fell quickly in love with the woman who would later become my best friend, my wife, and the mother of our children. After serving refugees in Austria for ten months as singles, Vicki and I returned to the U.S. to marry and, after a few months, moved back to Austria for another two years.

During our first year in Austria, we were privileged to meet Helena (a teenager at the time), her parents, her siblings, and many other refugees like them from the (then) Soviet-bloc countries, the Middle East, the Far East, and Africa. These were people who had suffered much, sacrificed much, hoped much, and dreamed much, and as a result, had much to teach us. Many were also amazingly hungry for God and open to learning about new life in Jesus. Helena was one of these very special people, and we felt an immediate bond with her, one that only deepened as she opened her heart to the Lord and as we developed a relationship as siblings in Christ. We're very grateful that she has continued to walk with Jesus, kept in touch over the years, and allowed the Lord to use her writing gift to help put this book together.

In the spring of 1990, I received a call from my leader John Swale asking if Vicki and I might be interested in starting a refugee ministry team in Athens, Greece.

"No thanks," I answered.
"Well," he said, "we have some research reports about the city that I would like you to read."
"I've already read them," I told him. "Interesting, but not for me."
"Well . . ." he tried again. "Some of us in leadership have been praying about it, and we think you are the man for the job.
"I'm very flattered. But keep praying, because it's not me."
"Would you at least be willing to pray about it?"
Being the spiritual giant I was back then, I responded, "No. We love our life, our ministry, and our team here. We have no desire to leave."
"Come on," he said, "you have to at least pray about it!"
"Okay," I begrudgingly replied. "But it won't do any good."

Two weeks later, God had changed our hearts from disinterested to enthusiastic. In June, 1990, we took our own research trip to Athens, and . . . hated it. It was in so many ways such a contrast to everything we loved about Austria. The pollution, the heat, the ugly, concrete jungle, the traffic, the lack of respect for the law, the disorganized and chaotic government, and the crowded city of five million people were huge turn-offs for us. However, there were countless refugees from a variety of countries, on whom no evangelical ministry was focused full-time. So we said, "Lord, if you want us to come, we are willing."

We moved here with our one-year-old daughter, Kendra, in September of 1990 with a commitment to recruit a team, build a ministry, and get out in two years. After eighteen months and only a couple more teammates, we started to pray, "Lord, where do you want us to go next?" We asked this question until 1995, when we finally realized God wanted us to stay right where we were until He made it clear that it was time for us to move on.

Four more children later and twenty years after arriving, we call this place "home," and we look back in amazement at what God has done.

We have not been alone. Slowly at first, but gathering speed as the years began to pass, the Holy Spirit led others from around the world to join our International Teams missionaries. People from Albania, Kurdistan, the U.S. and Canada, Greece, Iran, the Philippines, Australia, England, and Russia have been called by God to come alongside us and serve refugees who come mainly from Islamic countries in the Middle East, as well as refugees from Africa and Eastern Europe. Churches and individuals from Athens and from abroad have made personal and financial investments. Other ministries and parachurch organizations have formed various partnerships with us. We have had good leaders such as John Swale, Tom Albinson, and Jill Grage, who poured their lives into us and encouraged us when times were rough. It definitely has *not* been a "Lone Ranger" or "one-man show" kind of ministry.

Three things that drew us to refugee ministry in *theory* have kept us there for 24 years in *reality* . . .

1. Refugees coming from "closed" countries (mostly Islamic) generally become quite open to the Gospel in a "free" country where they will not be imprisoned, tortured, or (immediately) disowned or killed for asking questions about Christianity or for reading the New Testament. Many have moved from "seeking" to believing and receiving. You will read a few of those stories in this book.

2. Those who meet Jesus in Athens share Him with their friends and family who are also here in Greece, as well as friends and family back in their home country. *Most* refugees do not stay in Greece but move on to one, two, three, four, or more other countries before they are finally granted asylum, and they take Jesus with them. Some even return to their home country. The potential for "global impact" with refugee ministry here is amazing.

3. The opportunities we have (limited as they are) to combine the meeting of temporal basic needs with the sharing of the Good News of Jesus make an eternal impact on many who respond to God's love through His people. Both *proclamation* and *demonstration* are high values for us because we believe they are both highly valued by the Lord as He cares about us all as "whole" people.

Whether we offer showers and temporary shelter to refugees who are sleeping in the streets, or we have a seeker's Bible study after an evangelistic program; whether we invite a refugee family into our home for a meal, or we lead a weekend discipleship retreat for young believers. Whether we have a major clothing "give-away", or show the "Jesus" film to a room of 250 refugees; whether we teach an English or Greek class, or we give someone a Bible to read in their own language. Whether we give away sleeping bags, diapers, shoes, or baby formula, or we teach a weekly new believers' class. Whether we listen to a refugee's story, or we offer friendship evangelism, provide food to hundreds of refugees, or we simply pray with an individual—we seek to allow the Holy Spirit to work in us and through us to bring honor to the Father and the Son, to express His love for refugees through what we say and through what we do, with sermons and service, with words and works.

Our hope is that this book will encourage believers to know that God is at work in Athens, reaching the "unreached" nations (and reaching the people many consider "unreachable"). Our prayer is that this encouragement will lead to at least one of the three action points God calls His church to take: pray, send, or go. We hope that the churches and the individuals who have been partners with us for many years, as well as those who are learning about this ministry for the first time, will give praise to God for the way He is revealing Himself to the nations, and that they will also share the book with others.

This is an exciting time in history as God is bringing in a harvest around the world, especially among Muslims. What a wonderfully amazing opportunity to join Him!

This book is designed to be read easily, but also to be applied significantly. It is a great book to be read by individuals. It will be even more beneficial to be read, *discussed*, and applied in the context of *community*—in families, Sunday School classes, home groups, Bible study groups, prayer groups, school classrooms, mission schools, etc.

Most of the names in this book have been changed for security purposes. A few of the actual names have been preserved at the insistence of those to whom they belong.

Finally, it is important for you to know that every penny of profit from this book will go directly back into the refugee ministries of International

Teams. So, when you buy a book for yourself and for others, you are also supporting the ministry this book reveals. Without people like you who have supported the Athens Refugee Ministry over the years, we would *not* have a team in Greece. Our special thanks go to Lara Thompson Mobarez, Joanna Brenner Nash, Anne Perdicaris, and Sam Holdsambeck, who were present right at the birth of this book, transcribing the stories of our refugee brothers and sisters. We want to say many thanks to those who, at various levels, have already been an integral part of our team, and thanks to all of you who are about to join!

To God be the glory for the great things He has done!
Scott McCracken
Founder, I.T./Athens Refugee Ministry

Vicki and Scott McCracken – thank you for your friendship that opened the door to the Kingdom for this refugee.

Shirley and Cec Murphey – thank you for your love, wisdom and prayers that helped me see my purpose in God's Kingdom.

Introduction

When we receive information about refugees, it is often presented in terms of numbers and percentages. What statistics fail to convey is the depth of suffering these individuals experience on daily basis. The purpose of this book is to introduce refugees as people, only lost in the chaos of our world, who are much like you and me, trying to find hope and a future.

The stories of refugees connected with The Helping Hands ministry in Athens brought back many memories. It has been over twenty years since I have received my UN refugee status. Even thought the circumstances of my journey to the free world were not identical to the plight of millions of displaced people today, I felt a strong connection.

I identified with the desperate need to belong, to have a home, and to find a new hope for tomorrow.

I also understood the tremendous joy of finding a handful people who cared enough to invest their time and resources, offered help, but most of all their friendship.

Hearing the stories of refugees connected with Helping Hands ministry in Athens brought back many memories for me. It has been over twenty years since I received my UN refugee status. The circumstances of my journey to the free world were not identical to the plight of the millions displaced people today. I have never lived in a war zone, went without food, or had no place to sleep; yet I could identify with their desperate need to belong, to find a new home, and to renew their hope for a better tomorrow.

I could also share in their joy of finding a handful of people who cared enough to invest their time and resources, and who offered their help and friendship. Only later did I realize that standing behind the small group of missionaries are hundreds of faithful supporters who choose to give sacrificially and thus make the work of the mission possible. Most of them

I'd never meet at this side of Heaven, but perhaps this book is a way of saying thank you for changing my life. God knows your name, He knows your heart –you are changing His world for better –every day.

It was through the missionaries of International Teams that I heard for the first time that God loved me. They helped me to understand that language, nationality, and heritage didn't matter to Him. He sent Jesus to die for me, regardless of my citizenship status. His Kingdom reaches beyond borders and it thrives in the hearts of millions across the globe.

Vicki and Scott McCracken were key members of the I. T. team in Austria. We spent many hours together, learning English, reading the Bible, and discussing faith in Jesus. When my missionary friends explained that I was invited to join the family of God, I believed. From that moment on, I belonged.

I firmly believe that if we allow ourselves to see the refugees as people with names, families, and histories, as parents hoping for a better life for their children, and most of all, as our brothers and sisters in Christ, our world view will shift. We will no longer see the divide between us and them. Instead, we will understand that this world with its resources has been given to us to share. Statistics can be overwhelming and, truthfully, we can't help everyone, but we can be the catalyst of change for some. There is no telling what one changed life can accomplish for the Kingdom.

This book has been written out of the debt of my gratitude and as a gift to all who invested in the work of the Kingdom, so that missionaries like Vicki and Scott could fulfill the call on their lives and share the Gospel with lonely and desperate people, guiding them to the One who offers grace, love, and hope for the future.

Part I of this book will take you on a journey of a refugee—a true odyssey of our times—told by a young man from Afghanistan.

Part II is a collection of testimonies shared by refugees who passed through The Helping Hands Ministry in Athens. You will find that some stories stand on their own as a wonderful witness to the mercy of God and others are loosely connected by a thread of seemingly unrelated coincidences, allowing you to partake in the refugee journey toward hope.

Our prayer is that this book will be not only an interesting read, but also a starting point of many discussions among your family members, friends, Bible study group, or youth group. Please use the questions at the end of each story as kindling to spark your own dialogue and action.

Part I

1.

Home

Then he said to them, "Whoever welcomes this little child in my name welcomes me; and whoever welcomes me welcomes the one who sent me. For he who is least among you all — he is the greatest."

Luke 9:48, NIV

"From as early as I can remember, I have known nothing but sadness and trouble."

Hakim, Afghanistan

Hakim — Wise

I

My name is Hakim and I was born in Afghanistan in 1988. I am the youngest of four children. I know my father only from pictures. Though all my family were Muslims, my father was a committed communist. He lived in Russia and had been trained there as a pilot. After my three older siblings were born, my family lived in Russia for another six years. By the time I was born, my father was a high-ranking officer in the Afghan military, and he was head over all the airports in Afghanistan. He was of the Khalqi political party, while the president of the country at that time, Najibullah, was a member of the Parcham Party. He and several other Khalqi leaders were invited to Kandahar to attend a government meeting. En route, their plane exploded in midair. Fifty-seven people died, including several key Khalqi leaders. We believe it was no accident.

My mom somehow blamed me for being bad luck.

My mom somehow blamed me for being bad luck. Several years before my father's death, one of my mom's brothers, a commander of security guards in Kabul, had been gruesomely killed by the mujahedeen, Muslim warriors engaged in a jihad — a holy war. Now, her grief was overwhelming, and she was in no shape to care for a baby, so I was reared by my mother's parents. I became very close to them, especially to my grandfather. He was the strongest influence in my early childhood. I miss him very much.

I lived with my mother, my sister and two brothers, my grandparents, my mother's two brothers, and their wives and children. When we sat down to a meal, it was a large group of people. Sometimes it was quite noisy. I remember once that one of my uncles and his wife had a disagreement over disciplining one of their children. He told her not to beat the child but she did anyway. He then started beating her, chasing her all through the house. Another time, one of my aunts dared to gossip about my mother in the presence of one of her younger brothers. In defense of my mother's honor, she had boiling water thrown on her face, and you can see the scars to this day.

I was a very quiet kid, but I had some friends that I played with. We played with knives and slingshots, fighting against other teams of boys. I helped prepare the stones. Some of the boys even made their own "guns." At the arranged time, we would gather and shoot at each other, but because we lived in an area where there were terrible dust storms, you couldn't even see the other boys. If anyone got hit in the face, no one knew who threw the stone. It was a very rough game.

When I was nine years old, I broke my arm at school. A couple of older boys had been taken out into the school yard to be disciplined. We crowded around the window to watch their punishment, which consisted of being beaten with a rod on the bottoms of their feet. This was to set an example to the whole school. Since I was small and the window was high, I climbed up on the window sill; I fell backward and landed awkwardly on my arm.

I was raised Muslim, and my mother and grandmother considered themselves devout. We used to get up at 5:30 a.m. to go to the mosque to read the Koran at six. I used to pray to God and ask for His help when something happened or I wanted something. Sometimes I went to the mosque to pray. But to be honest, I only wanted to impress people and let them see what a good person I was.

He had a special book that he kept with his Koran. My mom believes it was a copy of the Injil [New Testament].

Although my grandfather wasn't a mullah, a Muslim trained in the doctrine and law of Islam and the head of a mosque, he knew the Koran better than the Islamic teachers. He had a special book that he kept with his Koran. He wouldn't allow anybody to look at it or touch it, but he would read it and kiss it, then carefully put it back. My mom believes it was a copy of the Injil [New Testament].

My mother's side of the family claims direct descent from the prophet Mohammad. When my grandfather went out in public, people came up to him and called him "Sir," and kissed his hand. He even had an official document verifying his genealogy. He was quite a character and loved making people think he was crazy by the way he dressed or the way he wore his beard. Yet he was highly respected by the people. He was a friend of the king, Zahir Shah.

In 1997, we moved to Mazar-e-sharif. We could have had a very good life if not for the constant fighting around us. There was always a cloud of uncertainty that hung over us. The house we lived in was nice. We had lots of land and hired help to care for five hundred sheep, goats, cows, donkeys, and chickens. Before we left, we sold all our animals to help finance our trip. My grandfather also owned a cave that had been fixed up like a house. I remember we hid there. I was scared because it was dark, and there were terrible noises all around us. A bomb was dropped near the opening of the cave, but, fortunately, it didn't go off.

The Taliban came to power, but the northern areas were not under their control yet. There was heavy fighting. We constantly heard the sounds of shooting. One of my uncles was a commander with the mujahedeen. Another of my uncles was a Talib. Amazingly, they lived under the same roof.

Most households stored weapons and munitions. In our home there was a shelf with a bread basket on it. It held eight hand grenades. One day, I was playing with my cousins, and we hit the shelf. The basket of grenades fell over and rolled on the floor. We could have been killed. My brothers handled guns on a regular basis; once, one of them fired the gun inside the house. The adults scolded him and said, "Go outside to play with that!"

Later that year, after the Taliban had finally taken control of Mazar-e-sharif, Hazara forces combined with Uzbeks and other groups, trapped and killed around five thousand Taliban soldiers. It was a terrible slaughter. There were rotting corpses in front of our house and in the streets. Blood ran everywhere. The dogs were eating the bodies. When I looked down our well, I saw at least fifteen bodies.

The new local government was now controlled by the Hazaras. When the soldiers arrived at our home, they banged loudly at the door, and then they rushed in. There was a lot of yelling and screaming. My grandfather held me tightly to his side. They forced us out of the house at gunpoint. I was really scared — I thought that they were going to kill us. They confiscated all of our property, but let us live. We briefly stayed at my aunt's home, and then moved back to Samangan.

> *Soon I understood that my two older brothers, ages nineteen and twenty-one at the time, had been kidnapped by the Taliban forces while they were outside. We never heard from them again.*

One day when I came home from school, everybody was crying. I asked what happened, but they wouldn't tell me anything. Soon I understood that my two older brothers, ages nineteen and twenty-one at the time, had been kidnapped by the Taliban forces while they were outside. We never heard from them again.

The Taliban regime was now in complete control. Afghanistan was a nightmarish place to be. My uncle who was a Talib told us we should flee. This uncle had actually been visited in Samangan by Mullah Borjan, a high-ranking Taliban member and close friend of Osama bin Laden. He came to thank my uncle for his service to the Taliban cause. I remember he presented him with a briefcase full of American dollars.

Once the decision to leave was made, things happened quickly. We sold all our livestock and many of our possessions. We buried a box under the floor of our house containing some important documents and pictures. We left in a great hurry at 1:00 a.m. There were thirteen of us in all, including my mom, sister, and me, my grandparents, two uncles and two aunts, along with four cousins. We made it to Kabul, then to Kandahar. We changed cars and drove to Pakistan. The next day, we arrived at Quetta. We lied to the border guards, telling them we were crossing the border to go to a wedding. They let us cross and our journey as refugees began. It was about a month past my tenth birthday.

• •

Rear-view Mirror

This is a story of Afghanistan told through the eyes of a ten-year-old refugee boy. How much evil can a child witness? Yet, God, in His ultimate mercy, can find a way into the heart of a small boy or a girl the same way he can penetrate the heart of a hardened man or grieving woman.

Through Jesus, God offers His love and salvation to our hurting world. He often does this through the work of missionaries and their faithful supporters, who dedicate their time and resources to His service. They fight evil on the front lines of His Kingdom, but these Kingdom fighters don't carry heavy weapons; their war is often waged on their knees, through tears and whispered prayers. Through His Son, God gave us the ability to reach out and help to rescue lost souls. Jesus came so that all of us may have life. He came so His sons and daughters would be able to find their way to our loving Father. Please, continue to reflect His image to this hurting world, and help the lost souls navigate their way home.

1. How unique, in your opinion, is this child's story?
2. What do you value the most about your home?
3. What is the estimated number of refugees in the world?

- -

Reflections

_____

_____

_____

_____

_____

_____

_____

_____

_____

_____

_____

_____

_____

_____

_____

_____

_____

_____

_____

2.

The Journey

And so I tell you, keep on asking, and you will receive what you ask for. Keep on seeking, and you will find. Keep on knocking, and the door will be opened to you. For everyone who asks, receives. Everyone who seeks, finds. And to everyone who knocks, the door will be opened.

Luke 11:9-10, NLT

As of the end of 2007, roughly one-third (an estimated 3,825,200) of all refugees and persons in "refugee-like" situations, as recognized by the UNHCR, were residing in countries covered by the UNHCR's Asia and Pacific region; 80 percent of them were Afghans. Pakistan (1.7 million), Iran (1 million), and Syria (1 million) host the largest number of refugees in the world. Taken together, these countries plus Germany and Jordan host 47% of the world's refugees. The Americas had the smallest share of refugees (9 percent).

2007 & 2010 UNHCR Statistical Yearbook

Hakim – Wise

II

Life in Quetta, Pakistan, was really not too bad. My uncles had jobs, we had a place to stay, and we had money for food. Then my uncles came up with a plan. The two of them would go to Iran because it is easier to smuggle individuals across the border than entire families. They would make money, and once they had enough to pay the smugglers, they would send for us. In the meantime, I was working in a watch repair shop, trying to make more money for our journey. As soon as we had enough saved up, it was time to leave Quetta. We acted fast. Our family took a long, hot, bumpy bus ride from Quetta to the Iranian border.

> *We were warned repeatedly to hold on tight because, if we*
> *fell off, the truck would not stop for us.*

The trip took thirteen hours. I was really miserable because I get very dizzy and sick riding a bus. At the border, we got onto a flatbed Datsun truck. We were warned repeatedly to hold on tight because, if we fell off, the truck would not stop for us.

Every leg of the journey we were given exact times of departure and were told that, if we were not there at the exact time, we would be left behind. I was always by my grandfather's side and even slept with him. He made sure I was always ready to go. At one transfer point, we were in such a rush to get on a bus that we had to leave our bags behind. We knew that when the signal to go came, we couldn't wait for anything or we would be caught by the police.

We crossed the border in the truck at night, without lights. It was very dark. The police found out about our transport and began a pursuit. I could hear them behind us, but somehow our driver outran them and made it to a prearranged hiding place. We stayed there for a long time while the police went by and searched for us. Finally, we made it to the town of Zahedan, Iran, and stayed at the smuggler's house.

The remainder of our journey to Tehran was by bus. Occasionally, it was boarded by the police, but we were never questioned or checked. It took us two months to get from Quetta to Tehran. We were lucky — for most refugees it takes much longer than that.

We all continued to stay together as a family throughout our time in Iran. We lived in a very large, very nice house, arranged for us by one of my uncles. We made many friends, since, as Tajiks, we looked a lot like Iranians. My uncles had good salaries, and the women worked at home making things for the market. Since we couldn't go to school, we kids spent our time playing and watching TV.

Two years later, my uncles, their families, and my grandparents moved to another house. My sister and her new husband, an Afghan she met in Tehran, lived with my Mom and me. This was the first time I had been separated from my grandparents. I was almost thirteen when I started to work at a factory learning how to make shirts. Then I worked at a big store that sold bulk containers of rice, oil, tea, and so forth.

In 2002, it seemed that the situation in Afghanistan was improving. My uncles and my grandparents wanted to return to Afghanistan, and so did I. We started to make plans to return. But my uncles decided to go back first and see. If the conditions were favorable, they would send for us. But my sister and her husband, who were expecting their first child, insisted on returning with them. At the end, only my mother and I remained in Iran.

> *Then we got a word from Afghanistan. It was no place for a widow and her thirteen-year-old son.*

It was a very sad and difficult time for my mother. She cried often. She was left alone with me, a son she really didn't know — who was like a stranger to her. Then we got a word from Afghanistan: It was no place for a widow and her thirteen-year-old son. Returning home was out of the question. My uncle told us that the only thing for us to do was to continue to Europe and find a place where I could go to school and get a proper education. My mom sold our apartment in Mazar-e-sharif. When my uncle came to Tehran and brought us our money, he arranged for us to meet an old acquaintance of his who was a smuggler. We moved in with this smuggler. He became like family to us. My uncle stayed with us as a guarantee that the smuggler would be paid. Once we were safely in Turkey, we would contact my uncle, and he would then take the smuggler back to Tehran and pay him.

We went to a Kurdish village in northern Iran, close to the Turkish border, and stayed with a family there. After about a month, we were put on another flatbed truck. I'll never forget it. It was a high, big truck, but it was very cold. We ran through several police checkpoints in this mountainous area. The truck stopped in a village and the smugglers took us to a house. They told us to get dressed in warm clothes. Then they put us on horseback in a caravan of about twenty horses. There was a lot of snow. The wind was very strong and we couldn't watch in front of us for drifting snow.

We rode at night for about six hours to the next Iranian village, a little closer to Turkey.

Exposed to the weather, we were extremely cold. Once the police left, we finally entered the village, frozen and exhausted.

We reached another small village, but were warned that the police were coming. Someone had tipped them off. The smugglers hid us on the side of a mountain. Exposed to the weather, we were extremely cold. Once the police left, we finally entered the village frozen and exhausted. We stayed there three nights. They fed us and cared for us, but we had to pay, as that was part of the deal. At any home we stayed along the way, we had to pay.

Then, the smugglers told my mother that we couldn't travel together. My mom bore a strong resemblance to the smuggler's mother, so he used his mom's passport and crossed the border with my mom in the car. She made it to the city of Van, Turkey, on the eastern shore of Lake Van. There she waited for me to join her. Her trip to Van was easy, but I almost didn't make it.

• •

Rear-view Mirror

Hakim, a young teenager, traveled for months and walked for days without proper clothing, food or shelter. But God was with him every step of the way. His protective wings kept him safe. Even before Hakim knew Him, God cared. Jesus died for him centuries ago, and He still loves him today. God chooses to show His love through people like us. Every kind gesture, selfless act, prayer, gift, volunteer effort — this is how God chooses to bless our world through His people. We have been chosen by Him to carry on the message of His Son, sometimes through words, but most often through our silent actions. Imagine God smiling as His children continue the work of His Son. Thank God for those who selflessly give of themselves to aid the hurting world, to help people just like Hakim to find the most important thing in their lives. Through their ministry many discover a new treasure, more valuable than any passport — the faith in Jesus Christ.

1. Look at a map and try to follow Hakim's journey. How many miles would you estimate he traveled at this point in his story?
2. Have you ever been in a situation when no one around you spoke your language? How did you feel?
3. List three ways people from diverse cultural backgrounds could make you feel uncomfortable. Why?

. . . .

Reflections

_____

_____

_____

_____

_____

_____

_____

_____

_____

_____

_____

_____

_____

3.

Fear

For you have not received a spirit that makes you fearful slaves. Instead, you received God's Spirit when he adopted you as his own children. Now we call him, "Abba, Father."

Romans 8:15, NLT

More than 18,700 asylum applications were lodged by unaccompanied and separated children in 71 countries, the highest number in four years. The applications came mostly from Afghan and Somali children

**2009 UNHCR Statistical Yearbook
UNHCR.com**

Hakim — Wise

III

My journey across the border was much more difficult and perilous than my mother's. It was winter and extremely cold in the mountains. The only way across was to walk. There were six of us, all Afghans. We followed our guide in silence as we sneaked by the checkpoints. When we crossed into Turkey, we walked through a small village. The guide went ahead and instructed us to follow, two by two, keeping an even distance between us. We were the first ones to go. We kept silent, careful not to make a noise. My heart pounded in my ears. I heard commotion behind me. "They got them. Look behind you," whispered the man next to me.

I looked back and saw that a number of large, Turkish policemen apprehended the other four refugees.

I looked back and saw that a number of large, Turkish policemen apprehended the other four refugees. They treated them very roughly as they pointed back toward the border of Iran, across the mountains. I heard them yell: "Here's the way to go. If you're lucky, you will make it. Maybe the police will catch you and send you back to Afghanistan. Or you will freeze to death and the wolves will eat you!" I was petrified.

The three of us walked as fast as we could. A car pulled up beside us. Because I was so small, they threw me in while the car was still moving. We drove for twenty minutes, and then stopped. The guide took us to a place on the side of the mountain. There we hid. We had some biscuits in our bags, but we had no water. I ate snow. We waited for three hours for the smugglers to come back. I wasn't afraid anymore because when I peeked out, I could see cars passing by on a big road.

When the smugglers came to collect us, they told us that it was not possible to make it to Van that day. We went to a house in another village. That night I slept near an oven called a tandoor, used for baking bread. There were also lots of chickens in this place, and the smell was horrible. But we finally warmed up and relaxed a little. As we talked, I saw a snake slithering on the floor. We killed it, but after that I couldn't sleep for the rest of the night. In the morning, the door opened, and we were given some bread, a very small amount of cheese, and two, tiny glasses of tea. After that, nothing. We stayed in there all day, without any other food except the biscuits we had in our bags.

We got out of the car and walked around the checkpoint. This took about three hours each time. The snow was very heavy and the wind fierce. I was hungry, cold, and exhausted.

Around 7:00 p.m., the smugglers came and took us on the next leg of our journey. They drove to the mountains. We got out of the car and started to walk. We walked for about eleven hours. The guide led us around every check point; sometimes we crouched low to the ground, sometimes we ran. At the next meeting place, a car with a new guide picked us up and drove us about twenty minutes until we neared the next police checkpoint. We got out of the car and walked around the checkpoint. This took about three hours each time. The snow was very heavy and the wind fierce. I was hungry, cold, and exhausted. The smuggler didn't give us any food or water, so we survived by eating snow and our biscuits, which we carefully rationed.

We got very close to Van, but the smugglers told us to wait at yet another hiding place next to a small river. My clothes were drenched by sweat from exertion, though it was very cold. I tried to tell the smugglers this in my language; they knew I was upset, but of course couldn't understand what I was saying. They told us that Van was very close and that we should be quiet. I was so tired I fell asleep. My companion was afraid I had died. He tried to wake me by hitting me and talking to me but I didn't respond. He was really scared that I was dead, and began to wonder how could he face my mother and tell her he was sorry, but I was dead. When the car finally came, he said, "Wake up!" To his amazement, I stood up and got in the car.

> *We were so tired we couldn't carry our bags anymore. They told us to leave them in the car as we trekked yet again around another checkpoint. We never saw the bags again.*

That night the smugglers told us that this was the last leg of the trip. We were so tired we couldn't carry our bags anymore. They told us to leave them in the car as we trekked yet again around another checkpoint. We never saw the bags again. We climbed over two hills, and then came to the third one. My companion said he couldn't walk any more. "If he can't walk," said the guide, "we will just leave him here. The wolves will take care of him." He tried to scare him, but my companion insisted that he couldn't walk anymore. I thought that I could not just leave him like that, so I turned around and put his arm around my shoulder, and we walked together. When the guide saw this, he came to his other side and supported him, making it much easier for me. We were in very deep snow, so the walking was extremely difficult. In some places, the snow was very hard on top, but in other places was soft and I would sink down in it. It was sort of like quicksand. The harder I tried to get out, the worse it got, or so it seemed. Finally, my companion became warmer and was able to walk on his own.

We knew we were getting close, and we were beginning to feel a little alive again. It was then that we heard the police dogs. Suddenly, it was like we had begun our journey all over again, as new waves of fear and energy came over us. We started running as fast as we could. We could hear the dogs barking but couldn't see them. Then the searchlights started. When the light came near us, we would stop and duck down, and when it left we started running. It was just like in the movies. At some point, the police stopped the chase and called off the dogs. Somehow, I can't explain how, we outran the dogs and made it to safety. We arrived in Van at the smuggler's house cold, hungry, and utterly exhausted.

After a few days, I was reunited with my mother. She was very close by, but we had to wait for a good time to be brought together. At this point, my companion wanted to continue on his journey, so he asked for his bag. They told him his bag was gone. In his bag he had several hundred dollars, many pictures and some very important documents that he hoped to make his case with. Of course, my bag was gone too. He was very upset and disappointed, but what could he do?

Even today, I sometimes see this man I crossed the mountain with on the streets of Athens. Once, when he saw me he said, "Do you remember that night? I will never forget that night! How did we ever make it? How could we have crossed such a mountain under such conditions?" We laugh and shake our heads in amazement.

. . . .

Rear-view Mirror

Fear is an emotion created to protect us from danger; it has the power to tell us when we need to hide, run, or defend ourselves. But fear can also become a most crippling feeling, preventing us from moving forward, making a decision, or saying the right thing. We all have experienced fear, perhaps not as intensely as Hakim, but we all can relate to his experience at some level. Fear can often be our enemy, stopping us from stepping up to what we know God has called us to do. The only solution is to pray and ask Him to give us clarity when it comes to our fears. Are those legitimate signs of imminent danger, or are those roadblocks placed in our path by our enemy, to deter us from seeking God's plan for our lives? Examine your fears, and pray that the Lord would give you strength to overcome them. Listen to His voice and follow His path, even though it might be really scary at times. Remember, He promised never to leave us or forsake us. Seek out His ways and He will lead you along the path, keeping you in His arms every step of the way.

1. Hakim was a thirteen-year-old boy left in the care of smugglers. What do you think went through his mind during this experience?
2. Think back to a time when you were really afraid. How did it feel? What did you do?
3. Visit www.iteams.org and overcome your fear of strangers. Choose a missionary and send them an encouraging e-mail this week

• •

Reflections

_____

_____

_____

_____

_____

_____

_____

_____

_____

_____

_____

_____

4.

Obstacles

Don't forget to show hospitality to strangers, for some who have done this have entertained angels without realizing it!

Hebrews 13:2, NLT

The UNHCR suspended its participation in the processing of thousands of migrants' asylum applications in Greece in protest of the provisions of a new presidential decree that would compromise the efficiency and fairness of an already cumbersome procedure. *"These new developments are likely to make protection in Greece more elusive for those who need it."*

Laurens Jolles, UNHCR Regional Representative
UNHCR Greece Press Review, 18–24 July 2009

Hakim — Wise

IV

My mom and I stayed in Van for one month. My uncle sent us some money, so we didn't lack for anything. I enjoyed my time there. I had a girlfriend and started learning Turkish quickly.

We lived in a nice house, had our own TV, ate good food, and had lots of nice things. In Van, we presented ourselves at a UN office to be officially accepted as refugees. After ten days we got the acceptance. They were going to send us either to Norway or Canada, but my mother didn't want to do that. She only applied so we could get the official refugee card. As long as we stayed in Van we were legally recognized refugees, but the minute we left, we were illegal again.

> *It was a very nice bus, but we had to stay in the bathroom*
> *of the bus with two other Afghan men, often for hours at a*
> *time. It was beyond miserable. We were sweaty and smelly,*
> *and there was no fresh air.*

We decided to go on. We got on a bus headed for Istanbul. It was a very nice bus, but we had to stay in the bathroom of the bus with two other Afghan men, often for hours at a time. It was beyond miserable. We were sweaty and smelly, and there was no fresh air. Periodically, they let us come out to sit in the bus; they brought us tea or whatever we wanted. One of the Afghans who spoke Turkish translated for us. They even had a waiter. It was very nice; I'll never forget it. This lifted our spirits considerably, and we spoke of our hopes and dreams for a better life. Finally, we made it to Istanbul.

Our living conditions in Istanbul were good. We had enough money to rent a nice house. We bought all the furniture and things that were in the house, including genuine Afghan carpets. But our goal was not to stay in Istanbul. We wanted to make it to Europe, to some country where I could go to school. We expected to be in Istanbul at least six months, but it turned out to be a stay of only about two and a half months.

> *Then he told me that he was the principal of the school at this*
> *mosque, where they taught English, French, Arabic, and of*
> *course Turkish. He suggested that I should come to school there,*
> *where I could learn to use the computer and most importantly,*
> *learn to study the Koran and become a mullah.*

I had several jobs in Istanbul. Once, I was waiting in the square to see if anyone would hire me for the day. A car stopped near me and the driver called me. He took me to work in construction at a big mosque, which also had a school for studying the Koran. Just before prayer time one day, a man approached me and started asking me questions about where I was from, my age, and so forth. By this time, I knew how to speak Turkish pretty well. He asked me how long I had been in the country, and when I said about two to three months, he said that he was amazed that after such a short time I could speak Turkish well. Then he told me that he was the principal of the school at this mosque, and they taught English, French, Arabic, and of course Turkish. He suggested that I should come to school there, where I could learn to use the computer and most importantly, learn to study the Koran and become a mullah. He said I didn't need to be working and should be in school. They would even pay me each week so I could buy the things I wanted.

I told my mother. When she heard "English," and "Koran," she said, "Let's stay, and you can go to school here." When I realized what was happening, I lied to my mother and told her that the car that had been coming to take me to the mosque no longer came. I never went back to get my pay check for that week. I didn't want to become a mullah. My mother was very disappointed.

I had several other jobs, such as making t-shirts and washing dishes at a hotel. One day, our smuggler showed up unexpectedly and, without really understanding what was going on, I found myself on a bus leaving Istanbul. We reached an area near the sea where you could see a Greek island in the distance. There were several people there who had been waiting for over a month for the right time to leave. We didn't even have time to finish our tea before a van came along and told us, "Hurry! Hurry! Get in, let's go!" It was like a bank robbery scene from the movies. Everything was always in a big rush.

> *The odor of petrol was very strong, and I was cramped with my knees against my chest. I wanted to throw up, and as the boat bounced up and down against the water, I either banged my head or my knees.*

The van took us to a speedboat. There were eleven of us, and because I was small, they put me up in the front under the deck. My mom sat in a comfortable chair by the helm. The odour of petrol was very strong and I was cramped with my knees against my chest. I wanted to throw up, and as the boat bounced up and down against the water, I either banged my head or my knees. But thank God, the trip lasted only about twenty minutes. Soon, we were dumped on the shore of a Greek island. It was completely dark. I don't even know what island it was.

My mom and I, along with another Afghan man, got separated from the rest of the people on the boat, who were Kurdish. We hid under a big bush until morning and then started walking. We wanted to turn ourselves in to the police. We signalled for several cars to stop, but nobody did. We walked about four or five hours on a very hot day — it was the beginning of summer. We had no water and no food, so we were extremely hungry and thirsty. The olive trees were just beginning to have some green olives on them and we tried to eat them, but that made us feel even worse. We were getting desperate. Finally, we came to a hotel and decided to go in and see if we could at least get some water.

I couldn't speak a word of English or Greek, but this other guy at least knew the English word for "water." We went into a beautiful hotel. A chubby Greek guy was sitting there, having coffee and smoking. He spoke to us, and my companion said, "Water, water!"

He motioned for some water to be brought to us. We decided to ask him to call the police so we could turn ourselves in. We gestured and made noises to communicate with him, and he said something like, "Problem, problem, no, police problem, don't go to police." He called his wife and two daughters, who were very kind to us. They gave us some coffee, my first cup ever, and some fruit. He asked us if we had any money, and my mom showed him all she had left — one hundred American dollars. He arranged for a taxi driver to take us to the port and buy ferry tickets for us. We were at this hotel for several hours, and we were overwhelmed by the kindness of this family. It made a huge impression on me. It was in sharp contrast to how we had been treated in the other countries we had been in along the way. I'll never forget the kindness of these people. They cried and hugged us when we left.

At the port, the dollars were exchanged to Euros and the tickets purchased. The taxi driver gave us our change — about five or six Euros. We thanked him and were going to leave when he said, "Hey, what about me?" My mom took off her gold earrings and gave them to him. He accepted them as payment. We boarded the ferry and started the long, overnight trip to the port of Pireas. It was the spring of 2003. I would be fifteen in a couple of weeks.

• •

Rear-view Mirror

Hakim's story gives us a unique window into the life of refugees, the world of smugglers, lack of basic provisions and constant fear of being caught. What propels people like him to risk everything, even their lives? It must be hope. Hope that there is a place, somewhere in the world that would offer them a better future. They seek a simple life, in which basic human rights are guaranteed by democracy; where food, shelter, work, and education are available to everyone. They journey for thousands of miles to capture their dreams, but when they arrive at their destination, they are faced with a rude awakening. There is no room for them. No one wants them. Although they see and even touch what they have been dreaming of for so long, it isn't meant for them. They enter a world of contrast, where there is no legal place for them. Many of them ask the fundamental question for the first time — what is the meaning of life? Why am I here? Why am I unwanted, rejected, ostracized, hated, blamed? Where do I belong? When these questions flood their minds and there seems to be no answer, their hearts long for God. He is the One who is calling His children to Him. He is the One who offers a permanent citizenship to millions of unwanted people. He is the One who stirs the hearts of His people to forget about politics for a moment. He sees Hakim, a teen that lost everything he had ever known and set out on a long journey seeking to belong. He has not chosen this life; it was given to him, perhaps as an opportunity for us, to live out our faith beyond our church walls.

1. How do you think Hakim felt seeing the tourist hotel, the beauty of the Greek island, the streets and stores around him, fully aware that his mother and he just spent the last of their money on a ferry ticket?
2. What contrasts have you experienced before that stuck in your mind?
3. What does the story teach us about evangelism?

Reflections

5.

First Encounter

For the Lord your God is the God of gods and the Lord of lords. He is the great God, the mighty and awesome God, who shows no partiality and cannot be bribed. He ensures that orphans and widows receive justice. He shows love to the foreigners living among you and gives them food and clothing. So you, too, must show your love to the foreigners, for you yourselves were once foreigners in the land of Egypt.

Deuteronomy 10:17-19, NLT

Interior Ministry of Greece is planning the creation of five new centers to accommodate thousands of undocumented immigrants by the end of August. Despite the fact that municipal authorities have drafted petitions, opposing the creation of "migrant concentration camps" in their region, the ministry is reportedly intent on pushing through the projects, which is sorely needed following the evacuation of the makeshift settlement in Patras and the Socratous Street squat.

Deal News 24 July, 2009

Hakim — Wise

V

After we arrived in Greece, we found our contact. He took us to a "refugee hotel" at Omonia Square in the heart of Athens. There were many Afghans there, as well as lots of Africans, but it was mostly single men, and it was definitely not an appropriate place for a widow and her fourteen-year-old son. I remember it smelled terrible.

A few hours later, he came back and took us to another "Afghan hotel." They had a small place up on the roof. It was then that we met a man from Mazar-e-sharif who went by the name of Navid.

> *Navid showed us kindness and said good things about life in Greece. The next day he brought us some potatoes and cherries.*

Navid showed us kindness and said good things about life in Greece. The next day he brought us some potatoes and cherries. I had a tape of Iranian music that I loved, and he let me use his tape player to listen to it. He told us that he had some books he wanted to show us, and it was then that we understood he was a Christian. He gave us these books, saying that they would help us understand more about the Bible and about God. We took the books, Mother took a copy of the Bible, and we said thank you. I didn't realize at the time what my mom was thinking, but she told me later that she believed that we would be able to read some of this material and then convince this man that he was going down the wrong path. This material was not the truth. Navid was terribly wrong and he was headed directly for hell.

Mom read the Bible a little, opening it at random to see if God would say something to her. She would read a page or two and put it down. I glanced at the beginning of the other books but quickly handed them to my mom, leaving it to her to look them over. She was not particularly impressed with anything at first.

We had to decide if we wanted to stay in Greece or not. One Afghan man we met wanted to help smuggle us to England. We were in contact with two of my cousins who lived in England. They talked with a smuggler, and I even colored my hair yellow in an attempt to disguise my nationality. Though we showed we were really serious about wanting to do it, our cousins began making excuses, saying that they couldn't trust the smuggler. The deal fell through.

> *We thought he was crazy. Here's this guy who brings us fruit and talks about Jesus all the time. He's really nuts.*

Navid continued to visit us and bring us food. He came so often it even started to bother us. He began to explain to us more about Christianity, and it was from him that I first heard the gospel — that Jesus was the Son of God, He died for my sins, and through Him I could have eternal life. We thought he was crazy. Here was this guy who bought us fruit and talked about Jesus all the time. He must have been nuts.

I remember when I was very young, one of my uncles on my father's side had a cross on a necklace. He had brought it for my aunt from Germany, where he worked as a policeman. I liked this necklace very much and wanted it, so according to the customs of our culture, they were obliged to give it to me. I wore this necklace with a cross on it while I was at their house, but nobody ever said anything about it or explained what it meant. Of course, I had no idea what it meant either. Apparently, neither did anybody else.

> *It was from Navid, a man from a town in northern Afghanistan where my family had lived, that I first heard the name "Isa Masi", Jesus Christ in Persian. I had traveled thousands of miles over the course of almost five years and never heard the name "Isa" along the way.*

It was from Navid that I first heard the name "Isa Masi," which means Jesus Christ in Persian. I had traveled thousands of miles over the course of almost five years and never heard the name "Isa" along the way. At first, it didn't mean anything to me. When we arrived in Greece, we saw all the churches, and we knew this was a Christian country, but we didn't know anything about Christianity. The symbol of the cross was a complete mystery to us. We had no idea what it meant.

Navid didn't say much to my mom, but he asked me to compare Islam and Christianity and see the differences. He knew the Koran pretty well and so did I, so it was easy for him to point out contrasts between it and the Bible. I remember one thing that bothered him was the language of the Koran. Why didn't they allow us to read it in our own language? Why did it have to be only in Arabic? Don't they want us to understand what's in it? I told him that I did understand a lot of what was in it, and he told me that I should know the Koran even better to compare it with the Bible. He said that I had a big advantage over other Afghans who were trapped in their ignorance and couldn't think for themselves. When he found out that my dad had been a communist, he encouraged me even more by saying that even my father was a smart person who knew there was something better than Islam.

I enjoyed Navid's company and the conversations with him, and I did a lot of comparisons between Islam and Christianity. But mostly my mind was preoccupied with what we were going to do. Would we leave and go to England? If not, where would we live in Greece and how would we survive? Navid was one of the few people who seemed to be interested in being friends with us. "At least while we are here," I thought, "it's good to have such a friend." But I was not giving serious thought to our talks because of the more pressing issue of survival.

Since we were having trouble getting our cousins in England to cooperate with us, Navid began suggesting that we stay in Greece. He told us about the Greek Council for Refugees (GCR), who would give us a house and money every month.

So, we applied with them and because we had a good case, we were accepted right away. When they offered us their congratulations that our application had been accepted, we thought they we going to put us in a house. Instead, we were given bus tickets for a refugee camp in Lamia in central Greece. Navid came to say goodbye to us and promised to stay in touch. He gave us his phone number and gave me his portable tape player. The next morning, with difficulty, we found our way to the bus station and went to the camp.

At the camp, my mom continued reading the Bible, trying to find things she could use to convince Navid how wrong he was. She read the Song of Solomon and was horrified by all the things about love and sex. She said, "Look! It's impossible for the Word of God to contain such things. I can prove to him that this is not the Word of God."

After we had been in the Lamia camp for a little over a month, Navid called us and said, "Why don't you get away from there and come to Athens and we'll have some fun together?" So we said, "Okay." He told us to save the receipt for the train ticket and we'd be reimbursed. When we arrived in Athens, we were running late. Navid met us and we hurried to a building downtown. It was the Athens Refugee Center operated by Helping Hands, where there were many Iranians and Afghans. They were having a church service! This was Navid's idea of fun? If he had told us why he wanted us to come we would have never agreed. An Iranian man was preaching and saying many things that were unfamiliar to us. It was incredibly boring to me.

They had taken our bags when we entered and put them in a small room called "the clothing room," used for giving away clothes to needy refugees. Later that evening we discovered all our clothes were gone. They had been given away. My mom was so frustrated and angry. The next time we were invited she didn't want to go. But they did give us money for the train tickets to and from Lamia each time we came.

. . . .

Rear-view Mirror

When Hakim first met Navid, he thought that the man was crazy. How else could he understand the love and kindness offered by a stranger? "Navid" means forgiveness, and in this story God sent one of His servants to minister forgiveness to this hurting mother and son. Navid's gifts of food and meeting basic needs opened the hearts of Hakim and his mother for God to walk in with His message of love and forgiveness. Perhaps his actions were the hands and feet of Jesus, ministering in a very tangible way to those in need. God's love was present when Navid brought a tape recorder to a teen that had been deprived of all that teenagers love, just so that Hakim could listen to his music. In the midst of a desperate situation, God found a way to bring a smile to a lonely teen.

Our Father cares deeply about us. He cares about the big stuff in our lives, but He also cares about the little details of our everyday living. Please pray today that His love would be made known to all.

1. What obstacles did Navid have to overcome to minister to Hakim and his mother?
2. Think back to your first encounter with faith. How did God find you?
3. On your errands this week, look for a stranger of a different background than yours. Bless them with a simple smile, or something more, if God leads.

Reflections

_____

_____

_____

_____

_____

_____

_____

_____

_____

_____

_____

_____

_____

_____

_____

_____

_____

_____

_____

6.

Provider

And my God will meet all your needs according to His glorious riches in Christ Jesus.

Philippians 4:19, NIV

Insufficient infrastructure and lack of specialized personnel, such as interpreters, lawyers, and social workers are two of the main problems of the detention centers at border areas, according to an interview of the Head of UNHCR Office for Greece Giorgos Tsarbopoulos on July 17.

Avriani, 24 July 2009

Hakim – Wise

VI

The second time we went to this church, the Persian Christian Fellowship, my mother was impressed by the love she saw in that place. People were kind to one another; they called each other, "brother," and, "sister," and talked to each other politely. By this time, she was no longer reading the Bible by opening it randomly; she was reading it from cover to cover. She knew all the stories of Abraham, Moses, and so forth. It was beginning to make sense to her, and as we were on our way back to the camp that night, she told me that maybe there was some truth to all this. Maybe this was why Navid showed such love to us. I was still quite fuzzy about it all, but when I saw my mother's openness, it helped me overcome my fear about possibly becoming a Christian.

Though this was only our second time to visit this place, I was already thinking about becoming a Christian. It was not because of any sense of guilt about my sin or understanding that Jesus died on the cross for me, but because I saw the love and warmth of these people and thought maybe they had something I didn't. I thought that maybe it would be a good thing to be a part of that. It was so different from anything I had ever seen before, whether in Afghanistan, Pakistan, Iran, or Turkey.

> *My mother had wanted to convince Navid he was wrong, but now she was becoming convinced herself. God was speaking to her through her reading of the Bible, which she was doing totally on her own.*

Conditions were crowded at the Lamia camp, but all in all, we were well taken care of there. The food was good, and we had everything we needed. I was able to work, and by the time we moved to Athens about five months later, we had saved about €2,000. After three months, our initial "white paper" that we got from the police had expired, so they took us to officially register, get fingerprinted, and get our "pink card." This made us legal in Greece for six months and officially recognized us as refugees.

My mother had wanted to convince Navid he was wrong, but now she was becoming convinced herself. God was speaking to her through her reading of the Bible, which she was doing totally on her own. I was not reading the Bible at all. Also, the love we received from Christian people was unlike anything we had ever experienced before. It made a huge impression on us. There had to be some reason these people were showering us with such love.

The third time we went back to the Persian Fellowship, we were ready to accept Christ as our Lord. We met with Navid beforehand, and my mom had several questions for him. He answered them in his characteristic way, with great enthusiasm and feeling, and we were satisfied with his answers. He told us that later that evening we would be asked to come to the front and they would ask us some questions about what we believed.

After the preaching was over, Navid took me by the arm and led us to the front. They asked us questions like, "Do you believe that Jesus Christ is the Son of the Living God?" Do you believe that Jesus died on the cross for your sins? Do you believe that Jesus is able to save you?" We answered all the questions and then they prayed for us and welcomed us into the family of God!

> *On the way back to Lamia that night, all we could talk about was how God had protected Navid, and how he had protected us all along our journey. It became clear to us that we had been prevented from going to England so that God could show us the true way of life.*

Soon we attended a special class for baptismal candidates. But we did not give very good answers to their questions. The leader told us that we weren't ready and there was no way we could get baptized that day. Yet he told us more clearly what it meant to be a Christian, and for the first time, I understood. We went with the group to the sea, not expecting to be baptized. But after talking to us some more and realizing our desire, they agreed to baptize us. They asked me to give my testimony. I was a little scared at first because I had never spoken in front of people before, but then the words just flowed out. I don't remember all that I said, but I'm sure I talked about comparing and contrasting Islam and Christianity, because that's a lot of what I was doing in my mind. I told them about how Navid shared the love of Jesus with us and how slowly I came to see the truth.

At this point, I had a very underdeveloped understanding of Christianity. I did believe that Jesus was God, that God existed as three persons, and that Jesus had died on the cross for my sins. But only in the months after that, as I grew in the faith, did I come to understand the concept of repentance and, apart from Christ, my absolute guilt before God as a sinner.

After the baptism, some policemen came to the beach. They called us over to show our papers to them. Navid said as we were going toward them, "Oh no, I don't have any papers!" He started praying and declaring the greatness of God. I think he was just trying to reassure himself, because he probably thought he was going to jail. The police then checked everybody's papers — except Navid's. It was a miracle before our very eyes. It made a very big impression on me and my mom. On the way back to Lamia that night, all we could talk about was how God had protected Navid and how he had protected us all along our journey. It became clear to us that we had been prevented from going to England so that God could show us the true way of life. We were amazed, and we rejoiced together at God's hand on our lives.

> *He told me he knew I was a good boy and that I should forget*
> *about the past and press ahead in my growth.*

After three or four weeks, we moved to Athens to live in "The Nest," a place for new believers and seekers operated by an organization called Helping Hands. Here we continued to see love among the Christians, spiritual discussions, and many other things that helped me see evidence I needed in order to strengthen me in the faith. I began attending Bible studies and learning many new things. Day by day, I understood more about Christ and Christianity.

But by the time the Olympics came to Athens that next summer, I had grown cold in my faith. I was doing some pretty wild things, like stealing things from shops and other shady activities. Up to that time, Navid had been the main influence in my Christian life, but now another man from Iran named Nader reached out to me.

He knew I was hanging out with some guys that were not a good influence. He asked me to come and talk to him, so we had juice together. I'll never forget that evening. He told me he knew I was a good boy and that I should forget about the past and press ahead in my growth. He invited me to go running with him the next morning, even though he was having many health problems. So, every morning, we got up at five thirty and went to the Acropolis or a big nearby park. We had great times talking and sharing about the scriptures.

Gradually, I began to invite some of the other kids who lived at The Nest to go with us. So, after running to the Acropolis, we would sit down to have juice and refreshments. Nader would hand me a Bible and have me read a passage and ask me to explain it. If I answered incorrectly, which was usually the case, he would help me see the correct meaning. During this time, Nader and I became very close and I really began to grow as a Christian. One of my old friends tried to get me to start hanging out with him again, but I wouldn't. I told him I had found a better way.

. . . .

Rear-view Mirror

Can God provide the seemingly impossible? A teen boy lost his way, with no father to guide him; yet, God found a man willing to step into his father's shoes and give of his time to mentor this young man. Had he said no to this calling, Hakim could have ended up in a jail, earning a criminal record, and thus losing any hopes for finding work or attaining a legal status in any country accepting refugees. Nader saw the need in Hakim's life and accepted the baton from Navid. God places into our lives the right people, at the right time. Our part is to be teachable and listen to the wisdom the Lord is sending to us through these men and women. God watches over us and sees into our hearts. When we feel lost, all we need to do is pray and ask, for He is faithful to come to our rescue.

As we progress on our journey through life and collect bits of wisdom and experience, there will come a day when He will call us to become a friend, a guide, or a mentor to one of His children. Just as Jesus mentored His disciples and then sent them out in the fullness of time to carry on His message. In turn, they mentored others to pass on the good news. As a result of this wonderful continuous chain, you and I are free to follow Him today. Hold firmly your baton, and in time, search for those who are ready to carry it on.

1. How can God be the father to the fatherless?
2. Who could you call a mentor in your life? Why?
3. Pray that the Lord would show you who needs your friendship, help, or wisdom this week.

· ·

Reflections

_____

_____

_____

_____

_____

_____

_____

_____

_____

_____

_____

_____

_____

_____

_____

_____

_____

_____

_____

_____

7.

Purpose

Do not come any closer," God said. "Take off your sandals, for the place where you are standing is holy ground."

Exodus 3:5, NIV

Greece pushes back people at its land border and sea borders with Turkey without first assessing their asylum claims. For those who do enter the country, there are many legal obstacles for refugees to gain protection.

Amnesty International
www.amnesty.org

Hakim — Wise

VII

I thank God that He provided Nader for me at that time. I was heading down a dangerous road, but he helped show me the way to go. I realized he was very sick, yet he cared for me, and God's love became more real to me through him. Though Nader didn't have much money, he always bought us juice and snacks and was willing to get up early and spend time with us. It was a very special time. Besides developing my relationship with Nader, I grew deeply in my relationship with God and in my relationship with the church.

One day, I was on the way to church, and one of the leaders was walking with me, talking about the story of Moses and the burning bush. Moses saw this bush that was burning but not burned up, and when he went closer to look at it, a voice told him to take off his sandals because he was on holy ground. I began to see that my experience in Greece had been something like that

Starting with the experience at the hotel on the island where we were shown such kindness, then God bringing Navid into our lives, who introduced us to the love of Christ, I realized that God was telling me to take off my sandals, because my sandals were my religion. Once I took off my sandals, it was like God said, "Okay, *now* I am going to talk to you." And all during that period when my heart was far from God, still God was working on me. So He brought Nader into my life to bring me back and focus me on the right way. I began to read the Bible for myself. As I was reading, I would ask God what it meant, and He would show me.

When I read the story of Moses, it was as if God were saying to me, "Because I have heard the cry of your people, I have brought you all this way for you to go back and free them." I realized that God had brought me through all these difficulties and had now brought me to Himself not for my own happiness and personal gain, but so I could go back to Afghanistan and tell my people the good news about Jesus Christ. This, I believe, is the call of God on my life. This is the ultimate result of my journey as a refugee.

> *Most members of our family back in Afghanistan don't know about our conversion.*

Most members of our family back in Afghanistan don't know about our conversion. My sister knows, and she accepts us in spite of the decision we've made. Some of our relatives in Europe who know we are Christians no longer have any contact with us. We haven't told other family members, not because we are ashamed or don't want to tell them, but we know they will reject us immediately and tell us never to call them again. Even if they were interested, for their own protection they would have to reject us and say bad things about us. We don't want to inform them of something as important as this over the telephone. One day, we hope to share the gospel with them face to face. We have a plan for how we would do that if the Lord enables us some day to return.

> *My life has changed completely since I've become a Christian. I'm aware of God's presence with me, and I communicate*

with Him in prayer. In Islam, for me, there was no sense of
personal communication at all.

My life has changed completely since I've become a Christian. I'm aware of God's presence with me, and I communicate with Him in prayer. In Islam, for me, there was no sense of personal communication at all. Because of the Holy Spirit within me, I'm sensitive to sins, such as lying and stealing, whereas before I didn't care about those things at all. I was full of anger and hatred, but now my heart is full of His love. Now my life is directed by the word of God, which tells me to respect and love my neighbor, not to look lustfully after women, and many things such as that — things that are not talked about in the Koran. Many of my Islamic ways of thinking have completely changed. For example, in a Muslim family, the head of the household is an absolute dictator and is only to be feared and obeyed. I no longer think that way.

Navid, my mom, and I were the first outspoken Afghan Christians in Greece, as far as I know. I lost many friends as a result of my conversion. We were well known among Afghans because we didn't care what any of them thought about us personally. We had accepted Christ, and He was our Lord, so popularity and acceptance among the people didn't matter to us. Only once did I suffer from any physical violence. A Pashtun man whose name I didn't even know saw me at the ice cream factory where I was working. We started talking and he asked me my name. When I told him, he said, "Oh, are you the one who became a Christian?" When I replied yes, he hit me in the jaw so quickly I didn't even realize what was happening. I never told my mother about it, but for one week I couldn't eat anything. I could only drink juice.

Probably the biggest discouragement in my daily life now is that we have not been able to get legal papers. The police lost our file with all our papers and our case claim. Since then, we have had a very difficult time. My mother applied for a green card over a year ago, but we haven't received an answer. It's a challenge to keep walking by faith in this discouraging situation.

It is so amazing to me how God has brought different men into my life at important times to help disciple me. It always seems to be just the right person that I need at the moment. He knows the way to take me and when to take me there. Sometimes at night, as I'm thinking about my life, I see the hand of God in so many ways, and I'm so thankful and amazed. It is difficult for me to explain. I am blessed.

One prayer request I have is that God would help me fulfill my vision of going back to Afghanistan, not underground, but to publicly proclaim the gospel and plant churches. My most immediate needs are to be able to go to college, and to get legal papers. Both of these things seem almost impossible. But with God all things are possible.

• •

Rear-view Mirror

It is only by the mercy of God that a traumatized child matures into a young man, filled with God's love and understanding of his own purpose. We traveled with Hakim as he left the horrors of war-torn Afghanistan, through the treacherous journey guided by smugglers, to a country that holds the illusive promises of better life, yet refuses to accept him as equal. Hakim's honesty offers us a rare opportunity to understand the refugee highway — the invisible road thousands travel every day, in search of a new life. What most weary travelers find at the end of this road are shattered dreams, as they realize that the world isn't interested in their plight. But there are also those who find the true riches of life. Their journey doesn't end in despair, but takes on another direction, following the new path of life, guided by a loving Father. Their problems don't disappear, their status isn't miraculously resolved, but they find hope. They see the hand of our God, the love of Jesus, the guidance of the Holy Spirit through the selfless actions of missionaries, volunteers, pastors, and hundreds of Christians who pray, work, and give so that the unwanted ones can feel that they are welcome. They are welcome to join us and become part of God's family, citizens of His eternal Kingdom that knows no borders, requires no passport or permit, and only asks that we freely accept God's love offered to us through the sacrifice of Jesus.

1. What is the greatest change we see in Hakim?
2. What is the calling, or the purpose, of your life?
3. Pray that God will reassure you as you follow His lead.

Reflections

Part II

8.

Another Traveler

Therefore, if anyone is in Christ, he is a new creation; the old has gone, the new has come!

2 Corinthians 5:17, NIV

The number of irregular migrants and asylum seekers detained last year on Greece's Lesvos Island after crossing from Turkey more than doubled from 6,147 in 2007 to 13,252, including thousands of children.

UNHCR News Stories,
19 January, 2009

Omid – Hope

I am from Iran. My father is seventy years old and has had three wives. I have six brothers and seven sisters. All of my brothers are in the army, and they are afraid they will lose their jobs because I left Iran. But my mind needs to be free. I have a free spirit.

I felt that I had lost something and had to go find it again — that is one of the reasons I left home. The other reason was to find a job. I didn't tell my parents that I was leaving. I only told my sister that I was going on a trip. For one year, I went from one city in Iran to another. In each place, I had a feeling that what I wanted wasn't there.

Life was very difficult, even though I found work each place I went. I applied for a passport, and after I got it, I went to Turkey. I stayed there for three years, trying to get to Greece from the first day I arrived. Then I was deported back to Iran.

It was a horrible situation, which lasted for nine months until I got a new passport, and then I went back to Istanbul.

I tried again to go to Greece. I told God I would do *Vuzu*, a bathing ritual, until I could get in. Good Muslims do this five times a day before prayer. I would do this after each time I went to the bathroom as well, remaining in a constant state of ritual cleanliness. I did this for a month.

On Christmas, 2001, I was in a square in Turkey where a Christmas program was taking place. When the program finished, I saw a black man giving out books. I was curious, so I asked him what kind of book it was. He said it was the holy Gospel of Jesus Christ. I didn't believe in Christianity, but I knew that the Bible is a holy book written by the prophets. So I kissed the book and left it on the street for someone else to take, since I couldn't read Turkish.

> *We inflated the boat. None of us could swim, but I didn't feel I was risking my life; I knew I would survive. God, who created the sea, could save me.*

A few weeks later, I came up with a plan. Four of my friends and I bought an inflatable raft. We planned to paddle from Izmir to the closest Greek island. I called my mom; it was the first time I had talked to her since I left. She wasn't happy with me, but I asked her to pray for me, since I didn't know if I'd ever see her again. We inflated the boat. None of us could swim, but I didn't feel I was risking my life; I knew I would survive. God, who created the sea, could save me and I had this confidence as I paddled.

We moved fast. After five hours, we arrived at the island of Híos without any problems. The police arrested us and held us for two days. Then they gave us red cards, indicating we were applying for political asylum, and 40 Euros, and told us to buy ferry tickets to Athens. It was so easy. On previous attempts, I had spent five days walking from Turkey to Greece. This time it only took five hours of traveling and two days in jail.

I didn't know anyone in Athens. Some Iranians I met told me to come to Helping Hands. The first time I came was on a Friday for shower ministry.

I was dirty from sleeping in the park. An Iranian named Nader was giving people shower tickets and told me I was very lucky because a lot of people hadn't shown up that day. I got to shower even though I didn't have a ticket.

> *"I know that one day you will believe in Jesus," he told me. I thought he was silly. It was impossible.*

I came back the next day for food and to watch the Jesus film. I loved it. A few days later, I looked up and saw Nader staring at me. "I know that one day you will believe in Jesus," he told me. I thought he was silly. It was impossible.

It is hard to find a place to stay in Athens. I found an empty house. It was open, so I went in. I stayed there for two weeks, coming to Helping Hands every time it was open, and going to a local church on Sundays. I went to church because I wanted to know what they were talking about. The first sentence I heard that impacted me was, "He is the God of love." When I heard this, I started to cry.

Two weeks after I moved into the empty house, two men, an Arab and an Albanian, came and told me that it was their house, but they would let me stay there. I knew that they were doing illegal things, but I didn't have any choice; I had no place to go. I thought that maybe God had put me there to bring the Albanian to church. I invited him to come with me several times, even though I wasn't a believer myself.

I kept a Koran with me the whole time. Whenever my Iranian friends asked me if I had become a Christian, I would pull out my Koran and say, "Would I carry this if I were a Christian? The only reason I go to church is to know what Christians believe." I was twenty-six years old, had grown up in Islam all my life. I had even done *Vuzu* for an entire month. How could I give up everything, as if it was all a game, and say Christ was the way? But in my heart, I knew. God was trying to show me His way by all these miracles happening in my life. But I couldn't accept Christianity. I said to myself, I have to know all the facts; I can't simply believe. I have to search for the truth for a long time.

One day, I went to church during a prayer time and prayed, "God, I'm tired, very tired. If You are real, reveal Yourself to me. I want to know You, and to know Your truth." That night I couldn't sleep. I prayed all night. I told God, "I only want to see Your truth. Open my eyes."

The next day, my friends cleaned the house. The Arab came and asked me, "Don't you have a Koran?" I handed it to him, and he read some passages out of it. Then he asked, "Do you know which direction Mecca is in?" I answered, "I don't know, but pray in four directions, and one of them will be right." So he did. I was confused because I thought that my Arab friend didn't believe in God. I soon found out that it was all a scam. He had stolen the Albanian's CD player and was planning to blame it on me.

> *Then I realized that Jesus was already changing me from the inside. My problems and bad characteristics were changing. I could tell He was working in me.*

That night, the Albanian invited me into his room. He asked me where his CD player was. When I told him I didn't know, he punched me three times, in both eyes and in the nose. My clothes were covered in blood. I told him, "I didn't do it!" but he didn't believe me. Thankfully I was able to escape from the house. I stayed out on the street all night before going to work the next morning. While I was working, I asked God, "You wanted me to bring them to Your church. What's going on? Why did this happen?"

But God was using them to bring me to Him. I had left all of my possessions, including the Koran, in the house, but instead of feeling sad, I felt free. Then I realized that Jesus was already changing me from the inside. The things that I did not like about myself began to change. I could tell He was working in me. It was as if God had punched me Himself to say, "Okay, you've heard enough. Open your eyes and listen to me!"

I had to look for a place to stay, but I didn't have any money for rent. I talked to some friends who said they had found a place where I might be allowed to stay and pay later. I was on my way to the appointment to discuss this when I passed Nader in the street. Nader said, "We hear that you need a house. We talked and decided to give you a bed in The Nest apartment. You can move in tomorrow."

I must admit, I had committed a lot of sin in my life. I had problems because of my sin. The devil would point to my sin and say, "That's you!"

But after I believed in Jesus, anytime the devil wanted to show how sinful I am, I could say, "I know, but Jesus paid the price for me." From the time I believed in Jesus, the devil has tried to make me sin more than ever. It has been difficult, because there are more opportunities than ever to sin, but now I have the strength to stand in Him.

What does the future hold for me? I love traveling, and I always thought I would make a good traveling businessman. Now, I want to travel for God, to go anywhere He wants me to go, to be His missionary. I was *baptized on June 9 at the local church I attend. I tell other refugees about Jesus. God has called me to a life of service for Him.*

• •

Rear-view Mirror

New life in Christ is perhaps the greatest miracle of all. The transforming power of grace and forgiveness has reconciled millions of souls with our Creator since the day Jesus uttered in agony, "It is finished." He has finished His mission on Earth, and provided a way to the Father for all who choose to follow Him. He also has commissioned His followers to lead the way for others, proclaim the Good News, and tell the world that the only way to the Father is to believe in Jesus Christ. The missionary workers and their supporters know that God will accept us, regardless of our nationality, our religious background, our past, education, social status, or wealth. These warriors for God know that Jesus came that we may have life, regardless of our Earthly citizenship. The gates to His Kingdom are wide open, and He is patiently waiting for His children to come home. Take a few moments this week and think of those around you and those who are in lands far away, still lost, seeking the way to the Kingdom. How can you point the way?

1. What issues do Muslim converts face?
2. Think of a time when you were challenged because of your faith by your family, friends, co-workers, or others. How did you feel?
3. Pray that those who oppose you would receive the Light.

Reflections

_____

_____

_____

_____

_____

_____

_____

_____

_____

_____

_____

_____

_____

_____

_____

_____

_____

_____

_____

_____

9.

Realization

And it shall come to pass afterward that I will pour out My Spirit on all flesh; Your sons and your daughters shall prophesy, your old men shall dream dreams, your young men shall see visions. And also on my menservants and on my maidservants I will pour out My Spirit in those days.

Joel 2:28, NKJV

"You need help not because you are poor, but because you are the future of Iraq."

Angelina Jolie
UNGoodwill Ambassador,
Baghdad, Iraq, July 23, 2009

Masun — Well Protected

I grew up in northern Iraq. In my early twenties I became a communist. My father was a fanatic Muslim. We always argued about God and His existence.

I left Iraq for many reasons, and I went to Iran. One year later, I left Iran and went to Pakistan. There I applied for political asylum. My claim was accepted by the United Nations, and they gave me a small monthly allowance, but my life was insecure. There are a large number of Islamic groups active in that area, and many of them invited me to their meetings and spent time with me, trying to convert me to Islam. But they were not successful. I never accepted the existence of God. My dream was to go on to Europe, get a job, and have a good life.

I became very sick. I was shaking and coughing; I had a fever, and I couldn't eat or drink. It was difficult even to swallow. My roommates brought me medicine but it did not work. I thought I was going to die.

Ten days after I arrived in Greece, I became very sick. I was shaking and coughing; I had a fever, and I couldn't eat or drink. It was difficult even to swallow. My roommates brought me medicine but it didn't work. I thought I was going to die. After seven days in bed, I had a dream. A voice said, "Open your eyes, and look up." In my dream, I opened my eyes and looked up. Somebody was standing there with a white robe shining bright around him. He told me, "If you want to get up from that bed, you should open your eyes and stop what you're doing. If you want to be healed, you should follow me." He showed me a beautiful garden, and He said, "If you want to experience this garden, you should be my disciple." I asked him, "Who are you? What is your name?" And He said, "I am the Christ. There is no other name in Heaven or Earth that can give you salvation but mine. Whatever you have, leave, and follow me. If you please the world, the world will please you. If you please me, I will please you." He said to me many other things, and at the end, He put His hand on my head and said, "Peace be with you." And I woke up.

A couple of days later, I woke up, and from my bed I told my friends again that I saw Jesus. I repeated everything that He said to me. I told my roommates that I promised Him that I would follow Him.

I was sweating and started to cry. Not from sadness, not because of pain, but crying with peace and joy in my heart. After I told my roommates, who were communists just like I was, they couldn't believe it. They said I had to rest because I must have had a high fever. A couple of days later, I woke up, and from my bed I told my friends again that I saw Jesus. I repeated everything that He said to me. I told my roommates that I promised Him that I would follow Him. Now I needed to find out from Christians how to do that.

I went to the Orthodox Church and I didn't find any answers. An Iraqi friend told me to go to the "American Church". So I went to Helping Hands and asked some questions. I asked what Jesus meant when He said, "follow Me." What did it mean to be a disciple of His? How can I be a good disciple? Who really is Jesus? How can I know Him better? What did my dream mean?

There was a worker from the short-term team and two other men; they talked to me about Jesus. They gave me more information and also showed me in the Bible the words that I heard in my dream. I had never read the Bible before, so I was surprised to see them in the book. I listened to what they were telling me about Jesus, and then I knew I had found my answers. When they offered to pray with me, I agreed. That day, I accepted Jesus as my Savior. I knew He was God.

Now I know there is a God and He loves me.

After our prayer, they offered to give me Bibles in the languages I could speak, so I could understand His word better. I asked if I could also have more Bibles for my friends.

The next opening day of Tea House, I brought my friends with me. I wanted them to hear the truth. All of us attended the Bible study and then stayed after to talk with the pastor about the Bible. He told us about the Persian Christian Fellowship.

I couldn't wait till Sunday. I asked my friends to come with me and they agreed. At the Persian Christian Fellowship I listened to the pastor. What he said about God was all new to me. I had never heard anything like that before. I was amazed that, although I have never read the Bible, God chose to speak to me in my dream. Now I know there is a God and He loves me.

• •

Rear-view Mirror

Discussions, arguments, fights — none of these can change man's heart. God has a different approach. He gently loves us and reveals Himself to us in many different ways. We can see Him in nature and admire the beauty of His creation. We can see Him in other people, and wonder about their selfless acts. He often enters our days unexpectedly and surprises us with blessings. He even steps into our dreams, when everything else is laid to rest. There He speaks directly to our souls. Perhaps He chooses this private time during the night, when all is at rest, to bring forth His truth to those who can't see it during the brightness of their day. At times our deep beliefs, customs, religious practices, and family traditions become stumbling blocks that are too hard to overcome. How can we, His creation, fully understand the Creator? Our imagination isn't great enough, our logic fails us, and our feelings are unable to encompass the greatness of His love. All that is left is sweet surrender. Our Father in heaven, hallowed be Thy name. Thy kingdom come, Thy will be done in my life today.

1. What are the beliefs of an atheist?
2. What was your conversion experience?
3. Pray for seekers who struggle to overcome traditions, religion, customs, and family expectations.

Reflections

_____

_____

_____

_____

_____

_____

_____

_____

_____

_____

_____

_____

_____

_____

_____

_____

_____

_____

_____

_____

10.

Questions

Ask, and it will be given to you; seek, and you will find; knock, and the door will be opened to you.

Matthew 7:7, NIV

Iran continues to suffer from double-digit unemployment and inflation (inflation climbed to 26 percent as of June 2008.) Most economic activity is controlled by the state. Private sector activity is typically limited to small-scale workshops, farming, and services. Unemployment among Iran's educated youth has convinced many to seek jobs overseas, resulting in a significant "brain drain."

www.cia.gov

Ferdows - Paradise

Even as a small boy growing up on an Iranian military base I dreamed big. My father served as an officer in the Iranian Army. We had an orderly life, filled with predictable days and practical goals. I was a good and ambitious kid, always doing what was expected of me. For me, ordinary life was a great adventure — running through the fields and racing through the soldiers' obstacle courses; I was a small warrior conquering imaginary enemies.

As I grew up, I became restless; confined in that military base, my dreams spilled over the walls.

As I grew up, I became restless; confined in that military base, my dreams spilled over the walls. Alone at night, I dreamed of leaving Iran and traveling to faraway countries. I also dreamed of victory, of freedom, and of great experiences. But beneath these goals was a deeper dream: to find my purpose. I was convinced that I would find it, if I could just escape this confining place. If only I were free, I could achieve success. I was driven by my dream and determined to make it real.

Every dream requires a first step, and my first step was to go to university. I graduated with a degree in English and then taught in Tehran. Soon, I'd saved enough money to take another step toward my dream, and I started to make arrangements to leave Iran. After four failed attempts, I finally crossed the border into Turkey. I headed to Istanbul, found a job, and met other Iranians who also dreamed of going west. We were young, energetic, and confident. Together, we planned our escape to Greece.

We took a boat and then walked for a week. The trek was exhausting. We were hungry and cold. En route, we were falsely accused of goat-stealing, and I used most of my money to pay off the accuser. Finally, we stumbled into Athens, rented a room in Omonia, a downtown neighbourhood, and set off to find work.

> *What did the future hold? Every day I wondered if I would forever be a refugee in Athens.*

Slowly, each of us found jobs and settled down. I didn't like being in Athens, though, so I kept myself busy working, learning English, and saving money to buy fake passports. Armed with these, I would be free to leave Greece. I bought the passports but needed more money for tickets, so I continued working. But my pay was so low that I really could not save any money. I was getting discouraged and felt that my dream was fading. What did the future hold? Every day I wondered if I would forever be a refugee in Athens.

During this time, a friend invited me to a Christian church. Having nothing better to do, I went. I didn't know much about Christianity, but, like most Muslims, I'd heard that Jesus was a prophet. To me, He was a myth — like Ali Baba. But as I walked into the church, I could see that the Christians had a very different idea. To them, He was real, and He was everything. I watched, amazed, as they praised Him joyfully and prayed to Him lovingly. They seemed to know Him as a friend, and yet they spoke of Him as God. Several told how Jesus had saved them and had given their lives a purpose. They called Jesus their Savior and their Lord. I was puzzled.

Their Savior? I didn't understand why these people needed to be saved, or how a myth could give them purpose. To me, the Christians' dependence on Jesus was a weakness and their enthusiasm was foolish. I looked down on their naiveté.

But then something happened that melted my defences: the pastor began to speak. He spoke of God in a way I had never heard. He spoke of Him passionately and pragmatically. First, the pastor said that God loves us. He read from the Injil, the New Testament: "God so loved the world that He gave His only son, so that everyone who believes in Him will not die but will have eternal life" (John 3:16). The pastor said that one of the names for God is "Abba," the Aramaic word that small children use to address their fathers. He said that God loves His children more tenderly than the most attentive father on Earth.

All of this sounded too good to be true. God loves me? God has good plans for my life? God wants to give me a future and a hope, and spend eternity with me?

He said that God is a good father who wants to give His children a wonderful life. He read from the Injil: "I came that they might have life, and might have it abundantly" (John 10:10, ESV). Like a good father, God has a plan for His children. "For I know the plans that I have for you, declares the Lord. They are plans for good and not for disaster, to give you a future and a hope" (Jeremiah 29:11, NLT). Furthermore, God loves us so much that He offers us the gift of spending eternity with Him in Heaven.

All of this seemed too good to be true. God loves me? God has good plans for my life? God wants to give me a future and a hope, and spend eternity with me? If God loved me and had a plan for my life, how could I feel that love and find that purpose? How could I become the child of such a wonderful Father? Perhaps, I thought, I never knew God's love and plan because I hadn't tried hard enough to please Him. Perhaps, I could become His child by working harder or by living a perfect life.

Yes, said the pastor, perfection was necessary. But none of us can be perfect. Even if we follow religious rules, perform good deeds, fast, and go on pilgrimages, we still won't be holy. We are sinners, said the pastor, and our sin separates us from God. The Injil makes this clear: "For all have sinned and come short of the glory of God" (Romans 3:23, KJV); "'There is none righteous, not even one'" (Romans 3:10, NASB); and, "All our righteous deeds are like a filthy garment." (Isaiah 64:6, NASB).

I had never considered myself a sinner. In fact, I thought I was a good person. But if good deeds couldn't save me and make me right with God, what was the answer? And then, as if by a miracle, I finally understood. Jesus was the way, and only He could bring me to the Father.

. . . .

Rear-view Mirror

Jesus became The Answer. But even when He prayed in the garden of Gethsemane, the answer He received from the Father wasn't the one He wanted. He knew it would bring Him excruciating pain, and, although He understood the importance of His calling, He struggled with God. In Matthew 26:42, we read: *Then he went away a second time and prayed, "My Father, if it is not possible for this cup to be taken away unless I drink it, let your will be done"* (NIV).

This is the beauty of our Lord, fully human, experiencing pain and struggle, yet fully God, understanding the purpose of these. He accepted the answer so that millions of others may live forever. He became the final answer to all our struggles, fear and pain. He gave us the privilege to be called the children of God. This gift cannot be earned by any means, but it is freely given. Please pray for the seekers who risk their lives, searching for the way to the Father. What a wonderful privilege to tell those who are lost about this wonderful Jesus, who loves them more than life itself.

1. What does the Koran teach about grace? What does the Bible teach regarding the same?

2. It is easy to get overwhelmed with the 'big questions' of our time. Find a way to become a part of the answer this week — volunteer, comfort, pray, donate — find your unique way.
3. Visit www.cia.gov/library/publications/the-world-factbook and read the facts about Iran. Pray for the people of Iran, as God loves each one of them.

• •

Reflections

_____

_____

_____

_____

_____

_____

_____

_____

_____

_____

_____

_____

_____

_____

_____

11.

Search for Belonging

He replied, "Because you have so little faith. I tell you the truth, if you have faith as small as a mustard seed, you can say to this mountain, 'Move from here to there' and it will move. Nothing will be impossible for you."

Matthew 17:20, NIV

In a "clean sweep" operation carried out on July 21, police evacuated the last, few, undocumented migrants from the premises of the old Athens appeals court in the city center. Most of the six hundred migrants who were living in the building had already left during the prior weekend under police surveillance. Alternate Interior Minister Christos Markoyiannakis announced a series of similar raids on occupied derelict buildings in Athens where hundreds of undocumented migrants are living in squalid conditions, some reverting to drug dealing to eke out a living. He said police would use "effective but safe" tactics to remove them.

Espresso 18 July, 2009

Jaweed – Eternal

I'm a Pashtun, and I'm from Afghanistan. I grew up in an area controlled by clerics and fundamentalist Muslims. I, too, was one of them until the clerics started to see all that I did wrong. First it was the little things, but my troubles seemed to grow with time. Things escalated until I was no longer safe in my home town, or even in my home country. I love Afghanistan, but I knew that I had to leave. So I did.

When I came to Greece, I worried. I was sure I wasn't welcome here. I felt loneliness, alienation, fear, sadness, and despair, and then depression set in.

Constantly on guard, I was scared of police and others who might cause me harm. I was an illegal alien, a person no one wants to see in their town — a paperless, status-less, country-less person.

One day I heard from an Afghani that Helping Hands gave food to people like me, so I came to see. He was right. I stayed for the meal. When the people who worked there started to talk to me, I wasn't sure what to say at first, but we talked a little and they smiled at me.

> *I felt good about the meeting; someone actually cared for me and honestly tried to help me, even though he was a Christian.*

I was searching for someone who understood me — someone who understood who I was and why I came here. One day, I came to Helping Hands to see Yaris, a staff member working at the center. I gathered all my courage and asked if he knew of a place I could sleep for a few days. He was very nice and tried to help, but had nothing available. But I felt good about that meeting; someone actually cared for me and honestly tried to help me, even though he was a Christian.

A few days later one of the workers, Stephan, asked me if I had ever read the Bible. It is not right for a Muslim to read that book, and I wasn't a Muslim in name only; I really believed. I was faithful to my religion and did live it out. But watching the Christians who made the meals, tried to help me with my lodging, and always treated me with respect, I wondered if reading their book was really that bad. "It would sure make them happy if I did," I thought. I told Stephan that I would read it. He gave me a New Testament in Urdu so that I could understand it well. He said we would talk about it after I read it.

> *From the time I was young, I was taught to hate everyone who was not Muslim — Christians, Jews, everyone.*

It's just a book of stories, I thought. But as I read questions came to my mind. From the time I was young, I was taught to hate everyone who

59

was not Muslim — Christians, Jews, everyone. We were taught that they wrote their "holy books" themselves to deceive others. Their books were not from God, but only from the minds of men. But somehow, the New Testament seemed different.

I came back to Helping Hands and started to ask questions. Every Tuesday, Thursday, and Saturday, I came to ask questions. I asked Yaris, Stephan, Nader, anyone who I could find. What they said made sense, and I felt satisfied. After weeks of questioning, all but the most important question remained. How was it possible that Jesus is both God and the Son of God? I was confused about why Christians believe He is God. Yaris gave a good answer, but I was not satisfied. I asked many others. Each gave me the same answer, but I still felt that things didn't connect.

One day, I went to listen to an Iranian pastor. I sat silently and prayed to God. I told Him that I was exhausted and weak. "You are holy," I prayed, "I want you to show me the truth. Please help me understand." I planned to question the pastor, but during the sermon, he repeated the answer everyone else told me. But that day, I finally understood.

When I read my Bible that night, something was different. It wasn't just a story anymore, especially when I read Luke; it filled me with a new feeling. For three days, I read Luke over and over. I saw myself in the story of the prodigal son. I, too, had strayed and had no way to get back to God.

> My heart overflowed with longing, emptiness, and sadness.
> My eyes filled with tears, and then I prayed. For the first time,
> I prayed to the God of the Bible.

It was 1:00 a.m., and everyone else was asleep. My heart overflowed with longing, emptiness, and sadness. My eyes filled with tears, and then I prayed. For the first time, I prayed to the God of the Bible and asked Him to forgive me. After weeks of searching for answers, looking for the truth, wrestling with all that I had learned and believed, I accepted I was wrong. God showed me He loved me. God loved Jaweed, the way he was. I knew He forgave me.

The next day, I had to tell Yaris that I had found the answer. He smiled, and from that day on, he called me a believer. He was my brother. I have lost my family, my country, my business, and everything that was once dear to me; but I have also received many things. I have God and the Holy Spirit. Jesus is with me. I will tell my family about Him, when the right time comes, and I pray that they will understand and look for the answers the way I did. At times, I thought I was out of my mind to come to Greece after my journey took me through so many other places, but now I know that it was a plan of God. If I had never come here, maybe I would never have known the truth.

• •

Rear-view Mirror

God can work miracles with a paper bag lunch handed out at the centre, gift of time, or a handful of change. In this story, a piece of bread, an egg, and three olives, given with love, radically changed a life. How many have been touched by the work of Helping Hands and selfless giving of many others? It is easy to feel overwhelmed with the needs of today's world. We can't solve these issues in our own strength, but with God, all things are possible. When one man searched for an answer to the most important question of his life, God already had an army of His people ready to reach out across the globe and meet his needs. God's love in action touched this man. He not only found his answer in God, but he also found a new family of Christians who, although he might never meet them in this life, are faithful in praying and giving so that others may know who Jesus is.

1. What was Jaweed's first experience with Christians?
2. How difficult do you find it to reach out to strangers?
3. Pray for peace, restoration, and safe return home for the Afghani people.

Reflections

_____

_____

_____

_____

_____

_____

_____

_____

_____

_____

_____

_____

_____

_____

_____

_____

_____

12.

Touched

The community is to have the same rules for you and for the alien living among you; this is a lasting ordinance for the generations to come. You and the alien shall be the same before the Lord.

Numbers 15:15, NIV

Almost one hundred officers and riot police took part in an operation on July 12, 2009, to clean out and flatten a makeshift camp for 2,000 irregular immigrants next to the port of Patras, which resulted in dozens of migrants being moved elsewhere.

UNHCR Greece Press Review, 11 - 17 July 2009

Rashaad - Wisdom

My family is Sunni (not Shiite), Muslim. I grew up in the Kurdish part of Iran. My parents were indifferent to religion, although they weren't completely irreligious. All of my family members were teachers. Because of that my only concern growing up was to do my schoolwork and earn good grades. Every summer, in line with our traditions, all young children in our town attended Koran classes taught by a mullah, and so did I, for seven years. I read the whole Koran three times during these classes. In addition, I have read books about our branch of Islam, as well as religious training books for mullahs.

Until I graduated from high school, I didn't have any problems. After I passed my final examinations, I thought about my life. I realized that, to me, God was somewhere far away from me, somewhere high up in the sky. I was here, down on the Earth, too far away from Him, and there was no way to connect with Him. I knew that many things in my life were sinful, but I couldn't stop doing them. I had no power to overcome my desires and stop being a sinner. That really hurt my faith.

I passed the admission exam to Tehran University and moved away from my family. That's when my real problems began. I became hopeless and didn't care about anything to do with God. Nothing I did bothered me. I enjoyed being a sinner. Sin became a habit, a daily part of my life. I didn't think about consequences, my future, or God. I developed emotional problems, then insomnia. After a few months, I couldn't sleep at all. If I slept, I would go to sleep late at night and wake up very early in the morning. I became sleep deprived. Looking back, I think this happened because my sin was bothering my conscience, but I didn't think about that then.

> *I wasn't allowed to do anything because of my political affiliation. I couldn't work. I couldn't study. I wasn't in prison, but it was just like living in a prison.*

I studied in Tehran for four years. In my third year I joined an opposition political party. Once the university officials discovered my political affiliation, I was expelled from the university and never received my degree. I wasn't allowed to do anything because of the political party to which I belonged. I couldn't work. I couldn't study. I wasn't in prison, but it was just like living in a prison. I stayed in Iran for nine more months, and then I decided to leave the country.

My plan was to go to Bulgaria, and then to England. I found contacts, and I had money and my passport. Everything was set. I made it to Bulgaria and stayed there for four months. My claim was accepted, and I was promised a Bulgarian passport. Then the events on 9/11 happened, and the law changed. My approved application to stay in Bulgaria was rejected, my application for a Bulgarian passport was denied, and I received an order to leave the country. I weighed my limited options and then decided to go to Greece with three other Iranians.

The first couple of weeks in Athens were very difficult. The weather was getting colder and we slept in a park. That's where I found out about a place the other refugees called "The American Church." Helping Hands was a place where we could get free food to eat. My friends and I went a few times and really liked it there. Later, we decided to help out. I received a Farsi Bible and started to read it. It was the only book I had in Farsi. At first I would read it just like a newspaper — it was just something to read. I didn't care much about the content; after all, I was a Muslim, and this book was about another religion.

After a few days, I decided to talk to one of the workers privately. He asked if I would like to attend Seekers' Class. I did. Then I received an invitation to Persian Christian Fellowship. A few weeks later, I was invited to visit another local church that my friends began to attend because they were interested in Christianity.

I really had nothing else to do, so to fill my free time, I went with them. I thought of what I heard, and logically, it all made sense, but I still couldn't accept it in my heart.

My friends and I went to Argos in southern Greece to work on a farm, picking oranges. There I met a new friend. He came from Bulgaria and spoke Turkish. He had been a Muslim, but he told me he converted to Christianity. We became very close. We worked together, ate together, and spent all of our time together. Every day and every night, during our free time, he read the Bible out loud to me. Before each meal, he prayed for all of us. His good attitude impacted me.

> *Before he left, he said to me, "Open your heart to Jesus. I will pray for you every day."*

One day, my Bulgarian friend came to me and said, "Tomorrow is Sunday. We haven't been to church in a long time. We should go together." I agreed. That Sunday, my friends and I traveled back to Athens because we wanted to take him to the church we had been attending. He prayed for us there, and while he prayed, he cried. When the work season was finished, he left for Bulgaria. But before he left, he said to me, "Open your heart to Jesus. I will pray for you every day."

Shortly after I returned to Athens, we heard of an opportunity to go to Italy. I left Athens and went to an island to board a boat. Everything was set, everyone was ready to go, but something held me back. I couldn't leave; I felt something wasn't right. I returned to Athens. I had no money. I was lost completely. It was the hardest time in my life. I had no idea what to do with my life, and then I decided to ask Jesus. All I said was, "If You are real, touch me."

On Thursday, I went to an Iranian fellowship at the church my friends attended. When I entered the church, I wasn't ready for what followed. I found the congregation singing and worshiping God. Then I felt something new in my heart, like it had completely changed. I felt different. I felt as if the words they sang were like a wooden board hitting me in the head, reminding me of my childhood. It was like a movie. I saw all the things that had happened in my life. I wept. My knees were weak, and I couldn't stand, so I knelt on the floor.

When I went back to our place, an abandoned, ruined building, I knew something was different. I rolled out my sleeping bag on the bare, concrete floor and crawled in. The floor was cold and hard, but I slept. For the first time in years, I slept through the night.

The best thing is that I can talk with my God directly. My God isn't far away, somewhere in the sky anymore.

Ten days later, I was baptized before my three friends who brought me to the church in the first place. My emotional problems disappeared. Instead, I had peace in my heart. Sin was slowly exiting my life as I lost the desire for it.

The best thing was that I could talk with my God directly. My God isn't far away, somewhere in the sky anymore. I know that my God is with me. He has a wonderful plan for my life here on Earth, and I'm very grateful for that. I don't know fully what that plan is, but I have decided to obey Him, step by step. I confess that He is the only one who can give us peace and that He is the only Saviour. I have the opportunity to leave Greece and live with relatives in another country, but I know that God is calling me to work in Greece. I have decided not to go anywhere until He tells me to go. Right now I'm a student again, learning each day, as He teaches me from His Word.

Rear-view Mirror

God finds us wherever we are — sleeping on a bare floor, sitting in class, or standing at the back of the church, hoping no one will see us. He is a relentless, passionate, and loving God who will keep knocking at the door to our heart until we either open ourselves to Him or send Him away. The miracle of God's love can melt the coldest of hearts, change the most stubborn minds, and heal the most deeply wounded spirit. God is Love — everlasting, ever-present, and ever ready to change our lives. What's most beautiful about this love is that it is always there, whether during the cold nights, days of hunger, or times of sadness, especially during the times we can't see it or feel it. At first, even before we know Him, it is a knowing in our soul. We suspect that there is something or someone out there, watching over us and giving our existence meaning. When we set out on our search to find that "someone," we begin to notice seemingly coincidental encounters with those who have already found the answers to our questions. And then, if our hearts remain receptive to the messages of love sent to us through these messengers, we begin to understand who the "someone" is. He is God, our Creator, who loves us and longs for us to love Him back. Send some of God's love today to someone who still needs to find Him — a prayer, a kind word, or a smile — just to let them know that God is waiting.

1. What was Rashaad's greatest need?
2. Think of a time when God's love surprised you.
3. Love one another — how can we extend Jesus' message beyond our church community this week?

Reflections

_____

_____

_____

_____

_____

_____

_____

_____

_____

_____

_____

_____

_____

_____

_____

_____

_____

_____

13.

Longing

'Lord, when did we see You hungry and feed You, or thirsty and give You something to drink? When did we see you a stranger and invite You in, or needing clothes and clothe You? When did we see You sick or in prison, and go to visit you?

Matthew 25:37-39, NIV

Supporters of the extreme right reportedly launched attacks against migrants, journalists, and passers-by in Agios Panteleimonas square on May 26, shouting racist mottos and beating migrants throughout the night. Just before the incidents, the basement of the church of Agios Panteleimonas, which gives shelter to many homeless migrants, was mysteriously set on fire.

Eleftherotipia, 28 May, 2009

Kambiz - Gifted

My name is Kambiz, and I'm twenty-three years old. When I was young, my father was always telling me to pray. Early in the morning, it became my habit to go out of the house, to clean myself by washing my face, hands, and feet, and then pray.

I screamed for my family, then fell to the ground and dug with my hands in the rubble, trying to find them.

One Friday morning, as usual, I came out to wash before prayer. When I was ready to turn on the water, an earthquake shook the ground. Everything moved around me. I was petrified. Surrounding buildings fell down, and then the earth opened and swallowed most of the houses around me. There were piles of rubble everywhere I looked — not one wall was left standing. I screamed for my family, then fell to the ground and dug with my hands in the rubble, trying to find them. Moments before, they were sleeping in the house, and now they were buried under the debris. I cried and dug with my hands. I called their names, but I never found anyone. I lost them all. I would never see any one of them again. Our village was in a remote area, so it would take time before anyone could come to our rescue. Alone and helpless, I cried and cried, fearing that I would lose my mind. When the rescue teams arrived, they came from many countries. They dug in the rubble that once was my home and found my family. I didn't see their bodies; they only showed me a picture. All the dead were buried together. The earthquake took all my family and relatives living in our neighborhood in an instant.

> *There were many new houses and buildings constructed while I was away. It was a new town. There was nothing left of the place I grew up in.*

I had nowhere to go but Afghanistan because some of our extended family lived there. When I arrived, they thought I had lost my mind and decided that the best way to take care of me would be to find me a wife. Marriage didn't solve any of my problems. What I needed was to rebuild my life. I needed to find a way for my life to go on. I went back to my town in hopes of starting over. Everything looked so different. There were many new houses and buildings constructed while I was away. It was a new town. There was nothing left of the place I grew up in. Two of my uncles and I decided to leave, this time for Athens.

When I first came to Athens, one of the first things that touched me was a cross on top of a Greek Church. As I looked at it, I experienced a strange feeling. Somehow, I wanted to know more about this Christian religion. I found Persian Fellowship, visited two times, and decided not to go back. Then I had a dream about the Lord. I wasn't sure what it meant, so I returned to the Persian Fellowship and asked for a Bible. My uncles found out and strictly forbade me from going back, but they weren't able to stop my heart's desire. I wanted to know more about Christianity. For two years I have been reading the Bible I received from the church, and through reading it, I came to know Jesus.

One day, I was visiting some friends and found a small booklet on the floor. My friends said it was garbage, so I took it and read it at night. It talked about Jesus, and how He died for me. I read it and then prayed that God would show me the truth. At the back of the book were three questions. I read them over and over again. I searched for a pen and checked off the little box next to each question. There was an address stamped on the back cover of the booklet, so I decided to mail it back to Helping Hands. I wanted them to know that I wanted to learn more about Jesus. To introduce myself, and to make sure they knew who I was, I copied my papers. I also sent a copy of the voucher for our house maintenance that had our address on it, in case they wanted to find me. I wanted them to know where I lived.

> *When the pastor asked me afterward what my uncles would say when they found out I became a Christian, I thought of the Judgement Day. "On that day, my uncles can't save me," I said to him.*

Then I had that dream again. It was exactly the same dream as before: a man told me that I must be born again. For three days, I searched for the pastor of the Persian Fellowship but couldn't find him, but when I went to the service that week, he was preaching. At the end of the service, he asked if anyone would like to follow Jesus. I put up my hand, in public, no longer caring if anyone saw me.

The pastor came to me after the service. I told him about the Bible I received from his church two years before. I told him that I lived with some friends and my two uncles in an old building, and how my friends saw me reading the Bible. They called me names and swore at me, but what pained me the most was that they spoke bad words about Jesus. So I stopped reading and hid the Bible under my pillow. I waited for them to fall asleep and then read my Bible with a small flashlight. When the pastor asked me afterward what my uncles would say when they found out I became a Christian, I thought of the Judgement Day. "On that day, my uncles can't save me," I said to him.

He told me to wait a moment. When he returned, I was surprised to see him holding the envelope I mailed to Helping Hands. He asked me if it was I who mailed it to the church. I nodded, and he embraced me. He asked if I would like to pray with him, and I did. We prayed for Jesus to come into my heart. Then he prayed some more. He asked God to guide me, to reveal Himself to me, and to keep me safe. When he finished, he said he would talk to his friend and see if they could find me a new place to live. I was overwhelmed. He embraced me and called me a brother.

On the day I was going to be baptized my uncle snuck into my bedroom while I was sleeping and poured boiling water on me. I stood before the church on that day, in pain, with serious burns on my arms and legs, and I proclaimed my faith in the love of Jesus.

While I was being baptized, my uncles changed the locks on our apartment and would not let me return. I found a new apartment, but soon after, someone set it on fire. My wife in Afghanistan learned of my conversion and divorced me, refusing to let our only child communicate with me. Yet I have peace and joy in my life. I live in Switzerland now. I have started a Bible study fellowship for Afghan refugees here.

$\bullet \quad \bullet$

Rear-view Mirror

Despair and loneliness are only two of many common issues among refugees. The men and women who travel thousands of miles in search of a better life often end up sleeping on the streets, in a park, or in overcrowded rooms in substandard housing. Hungry, cold, and sick, they hope that one day they, too, will be lucky and find a home in a country that will accept them as its citizens. Only a small fraction of them ever get to live that dream. But God finds His people even among shattered hopes. Through the tireless efforts of His followers, God finds a way to shine into desperate lives. Although the countries of the world may not accept them, He offers citizenship in His Kingdom. Through His Son, we are all equal in His eyes, and the gates of Heaven are open to all, if we choose to walk through and accept the gift of life Jesus Christ offers. This is the greatest miracle of all — in Him, we are all one Church, the Bride of Christ.

1. Can you think of a situation when a foreigner made you feel uncomfortable? Why?
2. How could you overcome your differences with this foreigner?
3. As members of one body, are we our brothers' keepers? What does that mean?

. . . .

Reflections

14.

Witness

God, who has called you into fellowship with his Son Jesus Christ our Lord, is faithful.

1 Corinthians 1:9, NIV

The amount needed to rescue people is less than what is needed to rescue banks.

UNHRC
High Commissioner
Antonio Gutteres

Rashid – Rightly Guided

I thought I was one of the lucky ones who made it all the way to England. I had crossed many borders in many different ways since leaving Afghanistan. I had heard so many good things about the life in England, and I was very happy when I finally made it. Until the police caught me. I was arrested and then deported back to Athens.

Life in Greece is difficult. I lived in an apartment with several other Afghani friends. It was hard for an Afghani man to get work. Without work, I had no money, not even for food. That is why I went to Helping Hands. I found out from other Afghans in the park that the people at Helping Hands give free food to refugees. I lined up and wondered what I would say if they asked me about my religion. How would they treat me? I knew they were Christians.

That day I was glad to get some food. It was pretty good. One of the workers invited me to stay. He also said I could watch a movie, if I liked.

That day I was glad to get some food. It was pretty good. One of the workers invited me to stay. He also said I could watch a movie, if I liked. I had nowhere to go, so I stayed. I watched the "Jesus" film and was surprised it was in my language. It had been a long time since I had seen anything in my language. As I watched the movie, I started to think about what I saw. I wasn't sure about many things, so I asked the worker to explain to me some more about Jesus. He talked to me, and then he gave me some literature so that I could read more on my own. He also told me about where I could find a Persian Fellowship.

I liked the idea of meeting other Afghani people and listening to someone speaking in our language. I started to come to the Persian Fellowship on a regular basis because I liked to discuss things about Jesus. The pastor also gave me a Bible. I read it and had more questions. He was patient, and always tried to answer all that I asked.

I don't really know at what exact moment I realized that I believed in Jesus. It just happened — one day I simply knew that what Jesus says in the Bible is the truth. I believed and started to follow Him.

Then he opened the window and said that the next time I brought any of these unclean books into this house, he would open the window and not only throw out the books, but also throw me out into the street below.

Some people think that life gets easy after they believe in Jesus. Not for me. I stayed with a group of Afghani friends who were all Muslims. I didn't tell them about my new faith. But one day, one of them searched through my things and found my New Testament. When I got home later that day, he was very angry with me. He asked why I brought unclean books into the house. I tried to explain, but he began to shout. I shouted back, trying to grab the book out of his hands. Then he opened the window and said that the next time I brought any of these unclean books into this house, he would open the window and not only throw out the books, but also throw me out into the street below.

A few days later, while he was out, I sat at our table and read my Bible. I was surprised when he suddenly rushed into the room and reached for my book. He grabbed it, waved it above his head and yelled at me again. He said that he had warned me already once about this unclean book. Then he grabbed me. He pulled me up from the chair and dragged me toward the open window. I didn't fight back, but prayed silently in my head. He shoved my head out of the window, so that I could see the street below. Then he yelled into my ear that he would throw me out, as promised. I looked at him and said, "If that would make you happy, you could do just that. But you need to know that God saved me. He changed me. He can save you, too. The Bible is true; it is not an unclean book." He stopped yelling. He stared at me and then let go of my clothes. Without a word he turned around and rushed out of the room.

> *It was a very powerful example to him. So powerful, in fact,*
> *that he decided to find out more. He went to Helping Hands*
> *to see for himself.*

Later he told me he was stunned. He expected me to fight back, to yell, to call for help, to be scared. He didn't understand how I wasn't afraid. He was shocked and wondered where I got the strength and peace in a situation that should make me scared. Was it really because I followed Jesus? What was this all about? What made me change so much so that I wasn't afraid to read my book and hold onto my faith, even though I knew there would be a lot of trouble for me in my house?

It was a very powerful example to him. So powerful, in fact, that he decided to find out more. He went to Helping Hands to see for himself. First he got some food, and then he started to talk to the workers. When one of them invited him to visit the Bible study, he said yes and started to attend on a regular basis. I knew God was working on his heart.

Later, he and an Iranian staff member started to talk about Jesus and the Bible frequently. It was very difficult for my friend to understand how God could come in the flesh. How could God become the person of Jesus? The most difficult question was how God could die for everyone's sins. But slowly, over time, as he continued to read the Bible and ask questions, he began to realize that Jesus could do all that. My friend understood that he too was a sinner and needed God's forgiveness and salvation.

It took him some time, but he finally decided to trust Jesus, and he began to follow Him, as well. In fact, he became so excited about his new faith that he decided to go to Iran. He was from Afghanistan, but his wife was Iranian and lived in Iran. He said he must go see her and tell her about the love he found in Jesus. At first, I wasn't sure he was serious, but he must have been; he left for Iran a few months ago. Last I heard, he was back with his wife in Iran, and that is where he is now. As for me, I live in Athens, praying and waiting for God to show me what He wants me to do with my life. I trust Him.

• •

Rear-view Mirror

Plans . . . often we think we know the best; we plan and plot; we try to find our way through life. But how do we recognize the difference between our own ambitions and God's call on our lives? How do we know that what we choose to do every day holds eternal value? It's easy to think that migrant people can't have a real purpose in life; after all, they don't even have a place to call their home. But what if we see the situation from a different angle? Is there a sense of community among them? Do they know of each other and track each other's progress?

How do they communicate? How do they live, without work permits, visas, and green cards? At times, their world seems so foreign to us that we fail to understand their needs. Rashid's story helps us to take a sneak peak at what their struggles are. How difficult the decision to follow Christ must have been for him! He knew very well that, by choosing Jesus, he would lose the last connections to his community. His life would change irreversibly. His friends would no longer accept him as one of their own. He was right. His life was put in danger, yet God miraculously intervened. Rashid's witness was so powerful that his friend needed to know what gave him this kind of strength. God used Rashid to minister to the needs of his hurting friend; and he, too, was welcomed to the family. Perhaps this was His plan all along. What is His plan for you today?

1. How could Rashid stay calm in a life-threatening situation?
2. Think of a situation in which God gave you strength to remain calm and in control, regardless of the circumstances around you.
3. Find time this week to write a note or an e-mail encouraging someone facing a difficult situation.

Reflections

_____

_____

_____

_____

_____

_____

_____

_____

_____

_____

_____

_____

_____

_____

_____

_____

_____

_____

15.

Prisoner

I needed clothes and you clothed me, I was sick and you looked after me, I was in prison and you came to visit me.

Matthew 25:36, NIV

In Germany, they came first for the Communists; I did not speak because I was not a Communist. Then they came for the Jews; I did not speak because I was not a Jew. Then they came to fetch the workers, members of trade unions; I was not a trade unionist. Afterward, they came for the Catholics; I did not say anything because I was a Protestant. Eventually they came for me, and there was no one left to speak.

Pastor Martin Niemoller, imprisoned during Germany's Third Reich

---

Ghodsi – Holy, Sacred, Angel

What I remember about our time in a Greek jail is that I was cold. I couldn't warm up. I worried about my husband, Dabir; the police separated us and took him to another part of the jail. I wasn't sure if they would beat him. He almost didn't survive the first beating he got in Iran. It was terrible; I was scared I would lose him. Dabir was a good Muslim; he only agreed to play at the Christian gathering to make some money.

When the police found out, he was arrested and severely punished. Was this Greek prison different from the one in Iran? What were we thinking?

I never thought we would leave Iran and all the persecution there, to end up in a Greek jail.

> *The first time I got in trouble with the government was when I wore the wrong color clothing. The second time, it was worse.*

I was a teacher. I taught Islamic catechism to women and children. The first time I got in trouble with the government was when I wore the wrong color clothing. The second time, it was worse. I was accused of teaching little girls to remove their head coverings. The truth was I was only checking their hair for head lice.

After the second incident, we decided to leave Iran as soon as possible. We headed west. When we traveled through Turkey, I had a strange dream. It was about Jesus. I walked behind Him as His servant. I was troubled by that dream, unsure what it meant.

> *While I sat in my cell, I wondered if I should pray to Jesus; after all, Greece was a Christian country, and He should have power here.*

It took us several months to get to Athens. I hoped that we had finally found a place where we could rebuild our lives. But I was wrong. Things got a lot worse for us. First, all our money disappeared. Then we were arrested. While I sat in my cell, I wondered if I should pray to Jesus; after all, Greece was a Christian country, and He should have power here. Later that night, my cellmate told me about her dream. In her dream, she saw four, great, shining angels surrounding me as she was praying. The angels also prayed for me and Dabir. Then the dream ended. Twelve days later both of us were released.

When we got out, we decided to find our only friend in Athens. I was surprised when our friend gave me a Bible in Farsi and the address for the Athens Refugee Center, the ministry center of Helping Hands. I couldn't stop reading. It seemed so wonderful. As I read many parts out loud to Dabir, he listened. I was thrilled when we found out that there were many Iranians at the A.R.C. who also believed in Jesus.

A few days later, Dabir had a dream. He dreamed that the Lord came to him, placed His hand on his head and said, "Follow me." He woke me up, excited, telling me about his dream. Then he said that he decided that he, too, must become a Christian.

> *And then Dabir sang. He sang from his heart about his newfound faith, he sang about Jesus, and he sang in our native Farsi.*

We didn't want to wait. We took the first opportunity to get baptized. On a sunny Athens beach, in front of a crowd of refugees and other believers, we confessed our Christian faith. And then Dabir sang. He sang from his heart about his newfound faith, he sang about Jesus, and he sang in our native Farsi. We got baptized together, as the crowd looked on.

Dabir and I have made a decision to serve the Lord with our lives. We enrolled in the International School of Ministry. Refugee life isn't easy. We don't have a permanent place to live, we aren't sure if we will stay in Athens or move on. We tried to start a family but had two miscarriages. We have a very hard time finding work. But despite our problems, I love being in Athens. We have lost everything, but we found Jesus here.

· ·

Rear-view Mirror

Even in prison, God sees His own. It's difficult to imagine what Ghodsi felt during those long days and cold nights in her cell. She was isolated from her husband, unaware of the particulars of the Greek legal system; she didn't understand the language; she was ignorant of her rights and frightened by memories. Yet God placed a witness into her cell. He sent her dreams of angels that showed Ghodsi in a very real way that He knew of her situation, and He cared. Please know today that God knows your situation as well, and He does care. Just look around and see the messages of love He has planted in your path. God has a plan. He sees the other side of the tunnel. Perhaps the difficult times are the most significant in our lives, because we are drawn closer to God. Our hurting souls long for the Father to hold us, comfort us, and assure us that He is still in control.

1. How did God communicate with Ghodsi?
2. Can you recall instances in your life when God has chosen to communicate with you in dreams and visions?
3. Google *sharia law* to gain better understanding of this story.

. . . .

Reflections

_____

_____

_____

_____

_____

_____

_____

_____

_____

_____

_____

_____

_____

16.

Dreams

He lifted me out of the slimy pit, out of the mud and mire; he set my feet on a rock and gave me a firm place to stand.

Psalm 40:2, NIV

The twenty-first century will be characterized by the mass movement of people being pushed and pulled within and beyond their borders by conflict, calamity, or opportunity. War and human rights violations are already scattering millions across the world in search of safety.

António Guterres, UN High Commissioner for Refugees

Zemar – Lion

I was an atheist. I didn't believe in any god, and I had a lot of reasons for my unbelief. But there was an empty place in me that nothing could fill. I realized I sinned a lot, and wanted to stop, but I didn't have the power to do that. Every time I would do something wrong, I would tell myself, "You said you would stop. Why are you doing these things?"

> *When I left Iran I hoped to find a better life. That was my plan, but God had another one. He brought me to Istanbul to meet Jesus.*

When I left Iran, I hoped to find a better life. That was my plan, but God had another one. He brought me to Istanbul to meet Jesus. As I traveled to

Turkey, my life constantly changed. I lived on the road. There were a few days of joy, but many more of sadness. I lived in Istanbul for two and a half years, and though I had money, I also had a lot of trouble in my life.

One day, I was walking on the streets with my friends when two Iranians came up to us and began talking about Jesus. It was Sunday, and I ended up going to church that evening. Worshiping God with joy and happiness was very strange for me. All of my life, I'd thought that God's way is full of sadness, and He will drag you far from joy. When I went back to the church, they gave me a Bible in Farsi. I started to read it. The miracles and the love of Jesus described on the pages made me cry. I had seen the same kind of love and kindness in other believers, and that drew me closer to their faith. They helped me, even though they knew I wasn't one of them. Those acts of kindness made me believe in what they said.

> *I felt like God had given me clean clothes to wear. That feeling kept me from sinning, because I didn't want to get those beautiful, clean clothes dirty.*

Since I accepted Jesus in my heart, He has changed my heart and life in many ways. My actions, thoughts, and words were completely changed. At first, I couldn't believe that it was possible, but I could feel that all of my sins were forgiven. I felt like God had given me clean clothes to wear. That feeling kept me from sinning, because I didn't want to get those beautiful, clean clothes dirty. From that time on, when I prayed to God and asked Him for something with all my heart, He answered my prayers.

One of the answers came when my father visited Istanbul on business. He was very old and frail and didn't know how to read or write. He didn't know that I believed in Jesus, and I was sure that he didn't know that Jesus is God. I prayed one night with my friends, asking God to show him and guide him, since he wouldn't accept anything from me because I'm his son. The next night, I was visiting with my friends, two other believers and a nineteen-year-old unbeliever. At about midnight, my father woke up and told us that he had an amazing dream. He said it was very strange, because he saw that a group of people put God on a cross. In his dream he asked himself how could anyone put God on a cross? It was impossible.

I asked him what God looked like. What had he seen? "He was a light, a very strong light," my father answered. We told him that Jesus was the Son of God, but he kept asking how a man can be God. Still, he went around telling everyone that he dreamed God was on a cross. He's not a believer — yet — but we keep praying for him.

The nineteen-year-old unbeliever sitting with us that night listened and didn't say much that evening. He came to Turkey because he wanted to go to the university there. He was in his last year of high school. A few weeks later he told me about a strange experience he had as he was going to class. "I didn't study for my exam," he said, "and I knew I wouldn't pass. I was afraid to fail, so I started to pray. I didn't know why, but I said, 'Lord Jesus, you know I can't pass this exam because I didn't study, but help me,' and then I started to cry while I prayed."

The most amazing thing was that this nineteen-year-old's father in Iran heard all these stories and accepted Jesus. He's now reading the Bible and going to church.

When he went to school to take the exam, the principal of the school found him and told him he was sorry, but they tried to get a hold of him earlier that day to let him know that the exam was rescheduled for the next week. Even though this young man wasn't a believer, he kept telling us how Jesus had helped him. The most amazing thing was that this nineteen-year-old's father in Iran heard all these stories and accepted Jesus. He's now reading the Bible and going to church.

From Istanbul, I planned to travel to Greece but I didn't know how. Two of my Christian friends and I wanted to go together, so we decided to leave on a Sunday evening after church. The day before, all three of us fasted, prayed, and asked God to help us. We asked Him to show us which way to go, where it would be safe to stop. We asked Him to be our leader, and we promised to obey. Saturday night, I had another dream. In my dream, someone told me not to go Sunday evening, but instead to leave on Monday morning.

I told my friend about my dream, and he was astonished. He also had had a dream that night. In his dream, we left Turkey on Sunday, but we got caught by the police. Because of the two dreams, we decided to try to leave Turkey on Monday afternoon.

It was amazing because with only a little money, within a very short time, without any difficulties, and only a day and a half later, we were in Athens. It was a true miracle. We thank God because that journey was a gift from Him. He helped us to come here. He is willing to help everybody. He helped us because we asked Him with pure hearts. When I gave my life and future into His hands, I believed that, in His hands, all of my problems would be solved. I don't know what will happen next, but I know that, wherever God sends me, He has a plan to use me.

• •

Rear-view Mirror

When we call upon the Lord, He answers. His Word promises us guidance and protection. He is faithful. So why do we struggle? Why are we faced with adversities and seemingly impossible situations?

Why is there injustice and suffering? Our world is broken. It is out of balance and tainted with sin. We witness abundant riches in the hands of a few, and mass poverty that plagues most of the world. The waste-producing lifestyle of developed countries contrasts with the lack of resources in the third world. How do we, His followers, live in this world? How do we minister to the less fortunate amidst our own struggles? We need to ask for guidance in our daily decisions. We ask for protection as we go about our daily business. And we need to learn to trust that He is faithful, that He sees our struggles, adversities, and difficult situations. As we renew our dependence on Him, perhaps then stepping out of our comfort zone and taking on new challenges might not be as frightening. Pray and ask the Lord to lead your way.

1. How do you think Zemar felt after he accepted Jesus?
2. Think of the time when you were a brand new believer. How did you feel?
3. Is there a miracle you need today? Tell God, and trust that He will answer.

Reflections

_____

_____

_____

_____

_____

_____

_____

_____

_____

_____

_____

_____

_____

_____

_____

_____

_____

_____

_____

17.

The Truth

"The King will reply, 'I tell you the truth, whatever you did for one of the least of these brothers of mine, you did for me.'"

Mathew 25:40, NIV

Iran has arrested about 70 Christians since Christmas in a crackdown... by Islamic leaders...The latest raids have targeted grass-roots Christian groups Iran describes as "hard-liners" who pose a threat to the Islamic state. Authorities increasingly view them with suspicions that range from trying to convert Muslims to being possible footholds for foreign influence.

Associated Press, January 11, 2011

Nader - Matchless

My name is Nader, and I was born in a small city in Iran. In the mornings, I studied to be an auto mechanic, and in the evenings, I attended high school. During my military service, I worked in forgeries making false documents, but I got into trouble for forging some papers for some friends, and I had to leave the country. From Turkey, I phoned my father who told me not to come back because a five-year jail sentence was waiting for me.

God, if I get out, I won't use drugs and I won't spend time with the Iranians who are bad influences on me.

In Turkey, I continued to forge documents and also started to use drugs. One night, I was using heroin when the police raided the hotel where I was staying with other Iranians. I was arrested, and after eight days in jail prayed, "God, if I get out, I won't use drugs and I won't spend time with the Iranians who are bad influences on me." The next day I was released.

I kept my promise. My time in prison had detoxified my body from the heroin, and when I was released, I could not find my friends. I worked at a job for nineteen months cleaning machinery by hand because the boss didn't have the proper chemicals. But I couldn't resist the temptation to forge documents again. I made a passport for Germany.

Before I had a chance to use the passport, I met an Iranian named Abraham who wore a cross necklace. I asked the man if he was a Christian. He answered, "Yes," and told me that he was attending an Iranian church in Istanbul. When I asked him how he had changed his religion, he answered, "I don't know how. God changed me." He encouraged me to read the Bible and to bring my questions to the pastor of the Iranian church. I stayed up late the night before going to church, smoking cigarettes and reading the New Testament, but I wasn't able to understand it. In the morning, I got up early to go to church, but as I looked in the mirror while shaving, I thought of God's great holiness and decided I needed to take a shower to "cleanse" myself. Suddenly the passages that I read the night before in the Bible made sense to me.

When I walked into church that morning, a believer named John approached me and asked if I was a Christian. I answered that I was. Then he asked me if I had been baptized. I thought of my morning shower and understanding the meaning of the Bible. "I was baptized in my house today," I told him. John looked at me strangely, but he and the pastor prayed for me. They told me that I really ought to be baptized again. Two months later, I quit smoking, but was still not baptized.

"God told us He wants you to go to Greece; pray and ask God."

I wanted to use my false passport to leave for Germany, but the pastor told me, "God told us He wants you to go to Greece; pray and ask God." Initially resistant to the idea, I eventually agreed to go to Greece with Abraham. Arriving with nothing, we slept in the park and began attending an international fellowship. There, I met a woman from the Philippines named Ella. She introduced me to Helping Hands volunteer, Joel. I had been a believer for one week at that time.

In Athens, I started growing stronger in my faith and helping with evangelism and practical service in the various programs. I was a house leader in our Nest Ministry. I was the primary leader of the Persian Christian Fellowship in Athens for many years. After I married Ella, the woman I met during my first visit to Helping Hands, we both officially joined the Athens Refugee Ministry team with International Teams in 2001. We continue to serve with them until this day.

We have been privileged to see many Muslims come to Christ while working in this ministry. I remember one night at Persian Christian Fellowship, during the worship time, I decided to show them the film, "Passion of the Christ." I chose that day to show the film because it was a holy day for Muslims.

When Jesus was beaten, one Afghan man went to the back of the room and sat on the floor, not able to watch the suffering of Jesus. Another one turned his face sideways, trying to avoid the scenes of beating. An Afghan man was crying and went to wash his face. At the end, another Afghan man said that he had been coming for two years just for the food. But this time, as he watched the, "Passion of the Christ," he was touched for the first time and asked if he could have a New Testament.

> *The next Sunday the same man came again, and at the end of the service, he asked to pray for salvation, saying he believed that Jesus came to pay the price of his sin.*

The next Sunday the same man came again, and at the end of the service, he asked to pray for salvation, saying he believed that Jesus came to pay the price of his sin.

I remember a refugee from Kurdistan. It was Tuesday morning at the Athens Refugee Center when he showed up looking for someone who could speak with him in Farsi. He said he had been a member of a political party in Kurdistan for four years and was trained to fight with guns for freedom. He had no interest in religion and God, but he was interested in new guns and new tactics for fighting. It took fifteen days for him to come to Athens with the help of smugglers who he paid six thousand US dollars. He stayed with other Kurdish people in Athens.

He told me he had a dream. In his dream, somebody was calling him. He looked up and saw writing in the sky he couldn't read. He heard again the voice calling him, saying, "Come to Me." He woke up crying and shaking. He told the other Kurdish guys about his dream, hoping they could help him understand. They told him to go to the religious people and ask them about his dream, and they directed him to our ministry center.

I was listening to his entire story, and I said, "I don't know what it means, but I know God is calling you to come to Him." I talked about God and told him that for many years, he fought for freedom and peace that he never received; maybe today was the time for him to receive it through Jesus — not by guns, but by faith in Him. I told him several verses in the Bible and he listened attentively. He took my hand and started to cry. He didn't care about the hundreds of people around us even though, for his sake, I tried to stop him. I gave him a Bible to read alone for himself and come back to ask any questions he had. When I was ready to leave him alone, he took my hand again and he said, "If I read the Bible and want to receive Him, what shall I do?"

I said, "Just open your heart and let Him come into your life." He said, "Can we do that now?" So we prayed, and he invited Christ into his life.

I was so happy and grateful to God for bringing this man to Himself. I was happy to see what God was doing in the hearts of the people. Then we prayed together, and he found the freedom in Jesus he had been searching for all his life.

. . . .

Rear-view Mirror

"We have an amazing God," says one of the volunteer workers at Helping Hands. "We are seeing the wonderful works of God among the refugees. He is always adding souls to be saved for His glory. Apart from Him, we can do nothing." Working in a mission field is a difficult task. There are many obstacles and challenges to overcome. The spiritual fight for the souls of the seekers unfolds on a daily basis, as missionaries are on the front lines of the Kingdom. There are often political issues that affect their work. The economics of a mission are directly dependent on the generosity of others. The life of a missionary is to be a life of complete trust in God. It is a life of service, humility, and love in action. It is also a life of great relationships — connecting people all across the globe. Missionaries link caring supporters on one end to the needy at the other. Missionaries are trusted conduits of God's delivery system. Please pray for the missionaries today, as they go on with their daily tasks, helping seeking souls to find their way to the Kingdom. Please pray for the supporters who are the backbone of every mission. Thank God for their faithfulness in selfless giving. They pave the road for the seekers to walk on. Also pray for those who are searching for God. Pray that God will guide their steps and place faithful people along their way who will point them in the right direction.

1. What role did the missionaries play in this story?
2. What does it mean to be a missionary? Does one have to travel overseas to be a missionary?
3. If you are not in direct contact with a missionary yet, find someone who needs your support this week. Learn more about what they do. Let them know you care.

Reflections

_____

_____

_____

_____

_____

_____

_____

_____

_____

_____

_____

_____

_____

_____

_____

_____

_____

_____

18.

Wife

A new command I give you: Love one another. As I have loved you, so you must love one another.

John 13:34, NIV

Early marriage, forced marriage, polygamy, high maternal and infant death rates, and the lack of education and job opportunities contribute to a bleak life beneath the burka.

Mary Kate MacIsaac
World Vision

Sabira – Patient

I'm from Afghanistan. My wife and our children are in Athens with me. We are one of the few families that are in Athens together. There are many more men here who left their wife at home, often with the children, hoping to make enough money to pay for their families to join them.

I want to tell you about a dream I once had. I dreamed about a small building. I couldn't tell if it was a church or a mosque, but there were two people standing there — one on each side of the building. I also saw a very bright light shining. It was so bright that I wasn't able to tell where it was coming from. I stepped closer to the building to see if the building itself was the source of the very powerful light. As I drew near, a voice came from one of those who were standing on one side of the building. "If you want to know about God, this is the way. This is the only way. This is the door you need to enter."

I didn't understand the meaning of this dream, but I thought that the reason I had such a dream was because many times I had wondered what the truth about God was, and what the true way to Him was.

I didn't understand the meaning of this dream, but I thought that the reason I had such a dream was because many times I had wondered what the truth about God was, and what the true way to Him was. I woke up excited, and woke my wife to tell her about it. She was upset and confused, and then she told me it was just a dream and we should go back to sleep.

My wife was pregnant with our third child, and we had no money. I worried about all the things a little child would need. We asked for help, and some of our friends told us about Helping Hands. So we went to see if they would help us with some items needed for the baby. Most of all, we were hoping to find a stroller my wife could use. Our friends told us that Helping Hands had given strollers to other families; perhaps we could get one, too.

While we were there, we talked to the workers. They were really nice to us and tried to help us out. We also talked about other things Helping Hands does for refugees, and I found out about the Persian Christian Fellowship. I must say, I was very happy to hear that there is a place where people gather and speak our language.

On Sunday, we decided to go. The pastor was talking about Jesus, and he said, "Jesus is the way, the only way, the only door to salvation." When I heard him say that, I was excited. I thought of my dream. I had been wondering all this time if my dream had been about Mohammad or about someone else. But when I heard the message that Sunday, preached so clearly, I began to wonder if it were possible that the dream had been connected to Jesus. I decided to wait and talk to the pastor after the service. We sat down and I told him about the dream I had several months ago. I also asked him if he could help me to understand the meaning of it.

I was surprised when he gave me a book. It was a copy of the New Testament. He asked that I take some time and read it myself. He said I needed to see for myself if there was a connection between my dream and Jesus.

I did take the book and started to read. I wanted to know. As I read, question after question came to my mind, so I would go to Helping Hands, find someone who worked there, and ask them. Then, I would go back home and study the New Testament again until I needed answers to more questions. And then I knew. I found what I had been looking for. I had been looking for the God who created everything and loves each person, even me. I had a lot of trouble with the Taliban back in my homeland, and also with prejudice and bad treatment from the Muslims in Iran, where I lived for some time. I had decided a long time ago not to believe in any religion.

When I accepted Jesus, I felt very happy. I found what I was searching for. My wife did not.

I thought that all I needed to do was be a good person who treats others well and shows love to others as much as he can. But, in studying the Bible and seeing Jesus for who He is, my view began to change. When I accepted Jesus, I felt very happy. I found what I was searching for. My wife did not.

She was upset with me. She couldn't understand how anyone could change their religion. Over and over she would tell me, "I'm not going to change my religion." I talked to her, showed her the Bible, and asked her to read for herself. She refused. I prayed for her for a very long time. I also asked my Christian friends to pray for my wife, so that she could see the truth. I would go to the Persian Christian Fellowship for the Sunday services, and I would also go to the Bible study and prayer meetings — there I would always ask for prayers for my wife. I talked to others about Jesus, and some of our friends came with me to the fellowship, but not my wife. She refused to believe. But we kept praying. I knew that God could do a miracle in her heart.

I was very thankful for my friends at the Persian Fellowship. They always gave me good advice about my wife, like the day I told them about the TV incident. See, since my wife wouldn't read the Bible, I thought I would sit in the living room and read out loud so that she could at least hear the Word. When I did that, she turned up the volume on the TV and began speaking even louder herself, just so that she could drown out my reading. I was very discouraged about this. So, at our next Bible study I asked, "What should I do? My wife isn't accepting Christ. She isn't even coming to the Persian Fellowship, or to the Bible studies. She will not even listen to me read the Word of God to her."

> *They said that, instead of telling her about God's love, I could perhaps try to show her. I had never thought of that before.*

I was surprised when the others gave me good advice. They said that, instead of telling her about God's love, I could perhaps try to show her. I had never thought of that before. How would I show her God's love and God's power? They suggested that I could show her that God really changed me by the way I behaved toward her. I needed to show her that God really changed me from the inside, so that she would see the change in me for herself.

I was very happy to see the smiles on their faces when, a couple of months later, my wife came to the fellowship with me. Since that day, she and I, and all our children attend regularly. But what touched her most was their visit at the hospital after our youngest child was born a year later. The members of the Persian church came to see her and the baby. They also prayed for them. She was impacted by their love, their warmth, and their sincerity. She kept telling me how much they prayed for her and the baby. She cried when she saw how hard the staff from Helping Hands tried to find clothing and baby things for our baby.

After she got out of the hospital, she came back to the Persian Christian Fellowship, and this is what she said: "The brother of my husband and other relatives live here in Greece. None of them came to visit. None of them called. None of them asked about our situation. But the Christians have always been with us, showing that they cared. They showed us love, not because they wanted to push me to Christ, but because they wanted to show that Jesus is love."

After that Sunday, she finally started to ask questions about Jesus. She said she wanted to know Him the way I and the other believers knew Him. She wanted to know the God who had the power to change me. And then, one day, she unexpectedly asked me if I would read the Bible out loud for her.

Finally, the Holy Spirit changed her heart and she accepted Christ. Now our whole family is growing together in the love and power of God.

• •

Rear-view Mirror

Sometimes it takes years or even decades of prayers for the souls of our loved ones to be saved. We pray that the Lord would soften their hearts and guide them to salvation. Sometimes we try to help, to speed things along. We hint, discuss, and argue about the spiritual world, trying to win the argument and thus convince our friends and loved ones that we are right and they should believe just the way we do. We are discouraged and frustrated when they slam the door in our face and dig in their heels. Is there a better way to show them that we care? How about practical, unconditional love? Living our faith by serving others and praying for them speaks directly to their hearts. Sabira learnt that lesson through encouraging talks and prayer with other believers. He was blessed with the change in his wife's attitude toward the Christian faith. How marvelous it is when husband and wife praise God together, united in faith, stronger when adversities come. What a wonderful witness genuine Christian love is to a woman who has been separated from her family, her support system, and her people. Love is most powerful when administered with patience and kindness.

1. How did Sabira try to help God? Why wasn't he successful?
2. Recall when someone showed you a Christ-like love.
3. Show the same love to someone this week.

Reflections

_____

_____

_____

_____

_____

_____

_____

_____

_____

_____

_____

_____

_____

_____

_____

_____

_____

_____

_____

19.

Refugee Life

Do not oppress an alien; you yourselves know how it feels to be aliens, because you were aliens in Egypt.

Exodus 23:9

Many have asked me why I quit my job in order to serve the refugees. I couldn't do otherwise. Either I would have to stop praying to God to send more workers to minister to the Muslim countries, or I had to get involved personally with the thousands of Muslim refugees that God has brought into my country.

Nikos, Helping Hands Ministry, Athens

Mubaraq – Blessings

I'm the oldest of three children and have two younger sisters. My father and mother were strict with us children, but also very generous. We knew that they loved us. Our family was very close.

Morocco is a Muslim country. Everyone I knew was Muslim. Before my father passed away, my mom was somewhat moderate in her faith. She would go out with a simple head scarf, wearing trousers. When I turned seven, she became more devout.

After my father passed away, she submerged even more into her faith. She would cover her face when she would go outside. In addition to her five daily prayers, she started to learn more about Islam.

I grew up praying each day. I went to the mosque every week; my mom would always send me by myself, because my dad wouldn't go. I stopped going to the mosque when I was about ten years old. When I turned nineteen, I started hanging around with my friends more, drinking, doing drugs, and so on. Then I got a good job and decided to return to my roots and go back to the mosque every week.

I started to dream about leaving Morocco when I was sixteen. At the age of eighteen, I decided to go to France and join the army so that I could obtain French papers. I had three uncles who had done that in the past. I wanted to follow their example.

During the time between 1981 and 1985, I felt I needed to leave and search for a new life. There was no democracy in Morocco. The government did a lot of bad things. There was bribery in the courts. The police weren't respectful of the people. I didn't want to become like them. It grieved me to see ordinary people being treated poorly.

About a year before I left Morocco, I had a dream that I was in a church. In my dream, the pastor asked me to sit and learn wisdom. I didn't want to, but my late father told me to sit down and to learn. I forgot about this dream until much later — the day I was in Athens, in a church, where God reminded me of it.

I had a good job in Casablanca, working in a steel plant. I worked there for five years, always planning to leave. The economy was getting worse, and so were the politics. I saved some money and looked for opportunities.

First, I wanted to go to Spain, but those plans fell through. A year later, I heard about a friend who had been in Germany and had been deported to Morocco. He knew of a way back to Germany and agreed to take me with him.

We first flew to Turkey and stayed there for one week. Then we crossed a river and landed in northern Greece. I remember we walked for three hours. Then we stopped for a short break, changed our clothes, and took the bus to Alexandropoli. There I bought a ticket to Thessaloniki. Two hours into the trip, the police boarded the bus.

They treated us like animals. Above one of the doors was written, "There is no God here."

I didn't have any papers, and I told them I was Palestinian. They brought four of us into the basement of the post office and left us there for fifteen days. After that, they transferred me to a small jail without windows somewhere in the mountains. The room was about two meters by five meters. There were four of us in there. They fed us only twice a day. I faked sickness so they took me to the hospital in the village.

When I was released, the police took me back to Xanthi and put me back in the basement of the post office. I stayed for the next three months. I did not see any daylight during this time, as the cell had no windows either.

The police and guards were very bad. They treated us like animals. Above one of the doors was written, "There is no God here." Three months later, they released me, with a temporary stay permit, allowing me to stay in Greece for one month.

I left Xanthi, and I came to Athens. I found my friend who I had traveled with before. He didn't get caught. Then I was able to call my mother and sisters and tell them I was out of prison and doing well. I slept in a Sudanese hotel for about two and half months. Finding work was very hard.

A friend of mine took me to Helping Hands. He worked there. I got some toiletries and food from there. It was the only place I could wash my clothes and take showers, so I became a regular visitor.

One day, I had a conversation about Christianity with Scott. I was with some of my Moroccan friends who spoke English and could translate for me. Although he answered my many questions, I didn't believe.

> *The employer wasn't a nice guy, so my friends and I left and found shelter in an abandoned hotel. There was no running water or electricity there.*

I was having a hard time financially so I decided to go to the islands to find work that winter. I found a job picking olives for fifteen days. The employer wasn't a nice guy, so my friends and I left and found shelter in an abandoned hotel. There was no running water or electricity there. We found other jobs picking olives during the day, but we would go back to the old hotel during the night. It was a really hard time. After a month, I decided to come back to Athens to look for work there.

I stayed for two months with some Algerians in an abandoned building. I still had contact with my friend who worked at Helping Hands. He shared with me about Christianity every time I saw him. I agreed to go to the Korean church with him. I went there because I wanted to learn English. They also served food two days a week.

A team came to visit from Korea. They stayed for one month teaching English classes every day. I felt like they were my family. I had a good time with them. They had a drum set there, so I played for them a few times. I always looked forward to the English classes. Then they invited me to Bible studies. I attended once a week on Fridays at the Korean church. I learned about Jesus there. I started to believe and was excited to learn more. Then I started to attend Arabic Bible study on Thursday evening.

One day, I decided to put my trust in Christ. After that, I felt very good. When I was in Morocco, I was kind of fearful. I lost that fear when trusting in God. I felt comfortable for the first time in my life. I continued to have Bible studies with my Moroccan friends and some Americans.

After I had been a believer for about four months, I decided to get baptized. I went with the Korean church to Corinth and was baptized there.

> Although my life is in many ways very difficult, I know my
> life is in His hands. I'm learning to trust Him.

I always looked for work and tried to save money to leave Greece. My dream was to go to Germany. I tried to go a few times but always failed. A few months after I was baptized, I started to feel it. I was tired all the time and was dizzy a lot. I went to the doctor, and he immediately sent me to the hospital. I went through a lot of tests and was diagnosed with Aplastic Anemia.

I was very sad when I found out. I felt sorry, not so much for myself, but rather for my family at home. I didn't want to die so far away from home. I didn't want to cause trouble for them and have them worry about me. I took my head in my hands and said to the Lord, "You are in control. You have a plan for my life, and I will listen to you."

I stayed in the hospital for three months and went through different treatments. I needed to have a bone marrow transplant. I'm still in Athens to this day waiting for the procedure. I have faith that it will happen in God's timing.

Although my life is in many ways very difficult, I know my life is in His hands. I'm learning to trust Him. I live at The Nest, a shelter ministry of Helping Hands. I became a house leader. The Lord has put a burden on my heart to share His love with others, so I am trying to do that in different ways and in different places. I help translate. I serve and talk with others at the ARC. I hope that God can help me to share Him with others like He used others to share Him with me.

. . . .

Rear-view Mirror

It is astonishing to what extend God will go to save a man's soul – Mubaraq from Morocco, dreaming about a life in Germany, imprisoned for months in Greece, meets an American in Athens, who introduces him to the Gospel that originated over 2000 years ago in Israel. Then God brings him to Korean Christians who accept him as a brother, teach him about God, and also English. Later following Arabic Bible studies, this man decides to accept Jesus as his personal saviour. Some may say all this was a series of coincidences, but others will see the hand of God, protecting, guiding, and preparing a way for one lost soul. How much did God care for this one man? How much does He care for you today? Your journey might not take you across the sea, into a prison, or a foreign country, yet your soul is of utmost importance to our Father. Talk to Him today, tell Him about your hurts and let Him heal your soul. He is ready to listen.

1. Seriously ill, still on the refugee highway, how can Mubaraq sound so content?
2. Where does your contentment come from?
3. Plan a movie night – watch a movie about refugees together.

· ·

Reflections

_____

_____

_____

_____

_____

_____

_____

_____

_____

_____

_____

_____

_____

_____

_____

_____

_____

_____

_____

20.

New Faith

For I was hungry and you gave me something to eat, I was thirsty and you gave me something to drink, I was a stranger and you invited me in.

Matthew 25:35, NIV

Statelessness is a massive problem that affects an estimated fifteen million people in at least sixty developed and developing countries. Statelessness has a terrible impact on the lives of individuals. Possession of nationality is essential for full participation in society and a prerequisite for the enjoyment of the full range of human rights.

UNHCR.com

Abida – One Who Worships

I'm sorry I can't tell you my full name; I fear for my safety and that of my family. I was born in Iraq. My father was a Kurdish rebel. For twenty-nine years, since I was six years old, I lived as a refugee in Iran. I married an Iranian girl, and we started a family. My three children are Iranian. I'm not. I tried to get Iranian citizenship, but I was repeatedly rejected. I applied for a passport, but my application was denied. I wasn't even allowed to leave the country, which refuses to accept me as their citizen. I couldn't buy a house, and I wasn't allowed to buy a car. I was not even allowed to work. For twenty-nine years, every three months I had to go to the police and re-register as a refugee.

I have no nationality, no country to call my home. I don't
belong anywhere.

I thought that if I went back to Iraq, I might be able to apply for an ID card. I took a great risk in returning to the country of my birth, but the Iraqi officials told me that there were no records of my birth. I was not registered as an Iraqi citizen; they had no idea who I was. So, they couldn't issue any documents to me. I have no nationality, no country to call my home. I don't belong anywhere.

Out of despair and the need to support my family, I left Iran — illegally. I walked for miles through rough terrain. On good days, I shared a horse, and I even paid a smuggler to get me across heavily guarded borders. Finally, I arrived in Greece.

When I came to Athens, all I had left were the clothes on my back. I was hungry, so I looked for a place that would provide food for refugees. I searched for a place to stay, and since I had no money to pay for accommodations, I slept in the park. Some friends I met there told me about a place they called "The American Church." I found out later it is called Helping Hands. They told me I could get food there. I went in hopes for a meal, but the first time I came, Alan, one of the workers, wouldn't let us in. The place was already full.

I didn't want to become a Christian, but Helping Hands gave
me a place to stay, even though I was a Muslim.

The next week, I tried again, and I was able to get in. The people who worked there treated me with respect, and I liked that. After a while, I started coming to help, and I became a regular volunteer. I don't know why, but something was prodding me to help. I was planning to go to Italy, but somehow it never worked out. So I started to attend a seeker's class. The teacher encouraged us to ask questions, and because I was curious about Christianity, we had several interesting conversations. While I was asking questions, I was also translating for others from Farsi, the language of Iran, to Kurdish, the dialect of the Iraqi region where I was born.

I didn't want to become a Christian, but Helping Hands gave me a place to stay, even though I was a Muslim. I was grateful that I no longer had to sleep in the park. My new home had a few rules everyone had to follow.

One of the rules was that we had to go to Bible studies and discipleship lessons, so I went obediently. I read the Bible. Then I started to pray, talking to my God, and I asked Him to show me the right way, the true way. I found reality in the Bible; it made much sense, so I started to believe in it.

> *But when I read the Bible, I discovered that the God of the Bible is a God of love. I was not afraid of Him.*

I can't say that something special happened in my life to change me. But I kept searching for answers, because I had been taught that, if you did bad things, God would send you straight to hell when you died. God was not a God of love, but of fear and wrath. I was scared of Him. But when I read the Bible, I discovered that the God of the Bible is a God of love. I was not afraid of Him. I chose the God of love instead of the god of fear.

I felt I needed to move on. I wanted to go to Italy and then on to another country and apply for refugee status there, continuing my life as any other person would. I tried to cross the border to Italy ten times. I tried different methods, different smugglers. I am convinced Alan's prayers prevented me from going to Italy until I attended the Timothy Project — a weekend retreat with other new believers held outside Athens. See, I had made Alan promise that he would pray for me, so that I could enter Italy. He agreed, but said that he would pray only after I came to the Timothy Project with him.

There I learned that being a Christian means I can have God close to me at all times. That gives me great peace. I haven't told my family that I believe in Jesus. If I told my parents, they would probably kill me. It's possible that the love of parents would keep them from killing me, but they would disown me from their family; so would my brothers and sisters. I don't know what my wife will do when I tell her. She is a very good Muslim. I think I can only tell my wife after she comes to join me in the new land, where we will live together again. I fear that she might not come if she finds out beforehand. Perhaps I will drop hints first before I tell her that I am a Christian, present her with all the information, and then let her decide.

God help me, I want to go to a country where I can live as a human being with human rights. I can't live in Iraq, because I have never lived with guns, and I can't live that way. I can't live in Iran, because I will never belong there. I want to live somewhere where I will have freedom, where I can live like a normal person. I want to bring my family there, legally, so that we can live in a real home, together, where my children can go to school and grow up in peace. I miss them so much. I used to be very depressed and sad because I'm away from my family for such a long time, but since I became a Christian, I have peace.

· ·

Rear-view Mirror

We all need to belong somewhere, to someone. We need to be a part of a family and a community. The need for relationship is at the core of our being; it is at the core of God's being, too. He created us so that He can have a relationship with every one of us.

It might take us many years to understand this wonderful reality, but once we do, no matter how far our family is or where our circumstances take us, we can be secure, knowing that God is never far away. He promised to never leave us. We belong to Him for eternity. Like the man in this story, we need to discover for ourselves that the God of the Bible is Love, and He really loves us. Abida now understands that he doesn't need to fear God. He doesn't need to be perfect or live a flawless life in order to please God and gain His approval. Abida found out that there is no way to earn mercy and salvation. All that we can do is to receive it as a free gift that was paid for by the blood of Jesus. Once we do, then we live out our faith by serving and honoring Him who loves us unconditionally.

1. Why did Abida not give us his real name?
2. What was his biggest struggle at the beginning of his journey?
3. What does the story teach us about friendship and evangelism?

Reflections

_____

_____

_____

_____

_____

_____

_____

_____

_____

_____

_____

_____

_____

_____

_____

_____

_____

21.

Justice

University teachers, human rights defenders, trade unionists and students are harassed, intimidated and detained. At least 346 people were executed in Iran last year by the state, including eight juvenile offenders. Death by stoning remains prevalent in Iran, and torture and ill-treatment of detainees is common.

www.amnestyinternational.ca

Naseef – The Just One

I grew up in an Islamic, religious family in Iran. I was doing all the things that were expected of me. As a good Muslim, I prayed five times a day, fasted during Ramadan, wept and cried on Moharam.

I was a chef in a fifteen-story hotel in Tehran for seven years. While I was getting divorced, I lost my job. I found a new job working for a mosque, making tea and watching the shoes of the faithful who entered the mosque barefoot.

Normally, I caught a bus to go home, but one day I started walking home instead. I was close to Tehran University when, suddenly, a large crowd of people spilled off the campus and into the street.

There had been a student strike, and the university forced the students off campus so the police could arrest them. I didn't know what was going on at that time. Police were everywhere. That day about five hundred students were arrested. Purely by chance, I was in the middle of it. The police separated men from the women, and put us in a prison. We didn't even know which part of Iran we were in. They kept us in the dark, and all we got to eat was bread.

> *When a policeman came in, he laughed at us. He asked what we preferred, to have our heads broken, or our fingernails pulled out. Then, one by one, the guards would come and take one person at a time to another room to be beaten and tortured.*

When a policeman came into our cell, he laughed at us. He asked what we preferred, to have our heads broken, or our fingernails pulled out. Then, one by one, the guards would come and take one person at a time to another room to be beaten and tortured. Some of the people taken never made it out alive. Others ended up in the hospital with severe trauma. Some simply disappeared. I prayed in my own language, not Arabic as Muslims are supposed to, and I called out to God, asking, "What's my fault? What have I done? Why should this happen to me?" On the twentieth day of my imprisonment, while I was praying, they called me into the interrogation room.

I knew I was going to die. I could hear women screaming. I was interrogated, asked what I had been doing there near the University. Every time they asked me a question, they would hit me. They discovered that I was simply a regular worker, and I didn't know anything. The university had security cameras all around its campus, and they could find evidence that would show me walking home. But they kept asking and hitting me, just to see if they could find out anything else. They were waiting for me to say anything, one word that would prove my involvement. They tortured me for seven hours. I knew this because, when they brought me in, the sun shone through a tiny window — it was straight up above, noon. When I thought they were finally finished, it was completely dark.

The interrogator couldn't learn anything of value from me. In his rage, he picked up a board. As he swung it toward me, it hit the light bulb that lit the room and then my head. As the light bulb exploded, I blacked out. I didn't know what happened after he hit me.

They moved me to the hospital. When I finally woke up, I found out which hospital I was in and that I had been unconscious for fifteen days. I wasn't allowed to contact any friends, and no one could visit me. After twenty more days in the hospital, I found a way to contact my parents. They came to visit me and told me that during the month I was gone they had been searching everywhere. The authorities let my parents come because, by then, they realized that I wasn't associated with any group.

> *Even though we tried, we couldn't go to the judge and receive justice for what had happened to me because the judge was also a part of the government. We paid a lawyer a lot of money, but he couldn't do anything.*

Even though we tried, we couldn't go to the judge and receive justice for what had happened to me because the judge was also a part of the government. We paid a lawyer a lot of money, but he couldn't do anything. The only thing the lawyer did was get my name off a list of members of some party that was in a lot of trouble, so that I could get a passport. To this day, I still don't know what the students were striking about. Through all of this, I still loved God, even though He let this happen.

Nine months later, I left for Turkey. I didn't have any money left after paying the lawyer, and I wanted to find a better job with better pay, so I left Iran. I have a nine-year-old son. I had to leave him with my parents. When I moved to Turkey, I saw a lot of bad places, and I prayed, "God help me, and protect me. Don't bring me there." God kept me safe and pure. Whenever I asked Him to do something for me, He would do it.

When I moved to Turkey, I met a person whose name was Amir. Amir invited me to go to church with him. I had heard something about Christianity in Iran, so I was curious to see the inside of a church. One Sunday, we went to the church. They were singing and dancing while they were worshiping. I had to take a step back and say to myself, "Oh, God will curse me," because I felt I also wanted to worship with song. In Islam, music is considered worldly, never to be used in connection with God. But I loved that kind of worship, and something wouldn't let me leave. I heard about the Bible. I heard that Jesus died for my sins, and that I don't have to play religious games for God to love me. I heard that I can worship God with all of my heart, and religious rituals didn't matter.

> *After they found out I was in a church, I still cooked for them, but they wouldn't let me sit and eat with them. They would just call for me to clean up afterward.*

When I came back home after church, my roommates found out where I had been. I had been cooking for all fifteen people living with me in this house. After they found out I was in a church, I still cooked for them, but they wouldn't let me sit and eat with them. They would call for me to clean up after they were done. All of my roommates were strict Muslims. I continued to cook for them for seven months, but never ate with them after that first visit to the church.

I was tired of their behavior, so I decided to leave Turkey and go to Greece. I had been in Turkey for almost three years. I arrived in Greece on June 21, 2001. It was on my second day in Greece that I met a boy whose name is Pejman. He brought me to Helping Hands where I met Brother Nader.

Nader told me about the baptism class because I was interested in getting baptized. I started to attend the class. The teacher was a man named Noel. I was in the class for two months, and then one day I woke up and felt I had received something in my spirit. I decided to get baptized. From that day, Helping Hands has helped me to grow a lot. I thank Brother Scott, Brother Nader, and Brother Themis.

My hope is to bring my son to join me and live under the power of God, no matter where, except in Iran. I want to be a servant. The only thing I can do is cook, so I want to cook for God — in Greece, America, anywhere, it doesn't matter.

> Note: *Naseef has a hole in his skull from being beaten in the head; he suffers from intense, periodic headaches. Despite this, he regularly volunteers at Helping Hands and cooks meals for the Persian Christian Fellowship every Sunday at the Athens Refugee Center.*

. . . .

Rear-view Mirror

God hates empty religion. When rituals and ceremonies replace a true relationship, we are left with an empty shell. What Jesus wants from His followers is their heart. When His people worship Him, it doesn't matter how beautiful their surroundings are, or what clothes the worshipers wear. What matters the most are their hearts and their attitudes. God loves when His people worship Him in honesty and truth. He also loves when we worship Him outside the church walls, with our daily lives. How do we do that? By living authentic lives, by keeping our promises, by doing what we say we would do; simply by being honest with ourselves and with those around us. That is how people will know that we are His children. They might not call us that; they might not even know what it is that makes us different, but they will feel that they can trust us. Naseef lived in ritual practices and did all that he knew to earn the favor of God, until he discovered the truth about Love. He found people he could trust. They kept their word, took their time, found a way to address his need, and then patiently explained to him that God already loved him; He was just waiting for Naseef to accept His love.

1. Why couldn't Naseef find any justice for what was done to him?
2. Have you ever been treated unjustly? How did you feel?
3. Look up www.amnestyinternational.com. Take a few minutes to browse the website.

Reflections

_____

_____

_____

_____

_____

_____

_____

_____

_____

_____

_____

_____

_____

_____

_____

_____

_____

_____

22.

Second Chance

For physical training is of some value, but godliness has value for all things, holding promise for both the present life and the life to come.

1 Timothy 4:8, NIV

The job of the police, the foremost goal, is to safeguard our border so migrants don't enter illegally, and as a consequence, to arrest them," said Anestis Argyriadis, chief of the border police in Alexandroupolis. Undocumented migrants are held in administrative detention for three months. Members of the European Parliament who visited one such center on Samos in June described its conditions as deplorable; it stayed open for another six months. The Greek Interior Ministry would not allow a reporter access to detention centers there or elsewhere.

The International Herald Tribune, February 26, 2008

Nur al Din – Brightness of the Faith

I am an Iranian. I must say, I was very deeply committed to an Islamic religion of meditation in Iran. We followed Ali, the son-in-law of Mohammad, and believe that Ali is the visible face of the invisible God. We honor him almost as much as Jesus is honoured by Christians. We see him in a similar way. I spent many years dedicated to praying and fasting in Iran.

Some might say that I was a fanatic Muslim in my particular branch of Islam, following our rules very strictly all the time.

I was also very athletic. We believe in physical wellness and combine sports and meditation. Some might say that I was a fanatic Muslim in my particular branch of Islam, following our rules very strictly all the time.

Nader and I first met in Turkey. Now he is a staff member at Helping Hands, but back then, about ten years ago, he was a new believer. I remember him telling me about his new faith in Jesus. I believe it was about a month after his conversion. I thought he had lost his mind. I couldn't understand how a Muslim could become a Christian and be so excited about it. I told him I wanted nothing to do with his new religion. I was so disturbed that while Nader was sharing his new faith with me, I felt a strong urge to get up from my seat and leave. I told him I had to leave immediately to go do the ritual washing before the Islamic prayer time, and then I left.

I had come to Greece and, for three consecutive years, I had been praying every day and fasting every other day. I had even memorized one third of the Koran. But all this religious activity had failed to satisfy me.

Now, ten years later, after Nader had come to Greece and started the Persian Christian Fellowship in Athens, I walked through the doors of Helping Hands, and there I see Nader. I was very surprised, and so was he. "Oh, Nader," I exclaimed, "I want to tell you all that has happened to me in these last ten years!"

I told Nader that I had come to Greece and, for three consecutive years, I had been praying every day and fasting every other day. I had even memorized one third of the Koran. But all this religious activity had failed to satisfy me. I wasn't sure what was wrong with me, but I knew things were not right.

My solution was to devote myself entirely to athletics. But even commitment to sports could not satisfy me. There certainly was a pleasure in improving my body and becoming more skilled, but it could do nothing for my spirit. I felt incomplete on the inside.

I was unable to find deep satisfaction in my soul. Nothing that I did brought me closer to God. I became very depressed and started to drink. At least alcohol could soothe my inner pain and emptiness, I thought.

*. . . no one would believe me. I was arrested, found guilty of
robbery and assault, and spent four years in a Greek prison.*

One night I became very drunk with some friends and got in a fight in
the middle of the street. The police came and arrested me and my friends.
The Greek man I had been fighting with accused me of trying to rob him.
That wasn't the case at all, but no one would believe me.

I was arrested, found guilty of robbery and assault, and spent four years
in a Greek prison.

In prison, I had a lot of time to think about the things that had happened
in my life. While there, an Albanian prisoner gave me a picture of Jesus,
which I put under my pillow. I would look at that picture every night
before going to sleep. One night I had a dream where Jesus, the same Jesus I
had on the picture under my pillow, was calling me to follow Him. I didn't
clearly understand the dream, but I was never able to forget about it.

After I was released from prison, I had nothing. I knew nobody. I had no
money, and I had no work. It is difficult for foreigners to find work , but
it is impossible for foreigners with a prison record to find any kind of job
in Greece. Then, some strangers told me to go to Helping Hands to find
food and clothing.

That was the day I found Nader. We found each other after ten, long years.
Although I was glad to see a familiar face, I found it very difficult to go to
a Christian for help. I felt guilty accepting help from Christians, so at first
I decided to refuse. But something kept bringing me back. Every time I
visited, I talked to Nader. And then one day, I just had to tell him. I had
to tell him about that dream I had in prison.

I was surprised when Nader sat down and smiled at me. He explained the
Gospel to me and how Jesus is alive and calling for me to follow Him. He
told me that Jesus wants to have a personal relationship with me today.
It was too much for me to understand. I had to leave. But every time I
decided not to go back, something pulled me toward Helping Hands. I
had all these questions, and Nader was very patient with me. He took
time, week after week, to sit down with me, listen, and give me answers.
I thought about what he said for days, and then I came back with more
questions. Several months later, after a lot of reading, studying, and many
discussions with Nader, I finally came to accept Jesus.

I must say, I am very excited about this new life that seems to satisfy the deepest longings of my heart. I found in Jesus what I couldn't find anywhere else. I feel an urge to tell others. I have to share with other Muslims this wonderful truth. I have to tell them how my life has changed and about the difference Jesus made in my life.

• •

Rear-view Mirror

Life is not an accident, and the people we meet on a daily basis don't cross our path randomly. There is a purpose in every meeting. Sometimes our encounter will end without any significant event, but there are times when we form strong connections with perfect strangers.

The relationship can grow with time until we develop a lifelong bond. Often, we don't know why we feel differently about certain people, but God in His wisdom sees the future. When Nur al Din and Nader met for the first time, they connected. Nader tried to tell his friend about God, but he wasn't ready at that time. But Nader's prayers didn't go unanswered. It took ten years for these men to reunite. Regardless of the time that had passed, Nader's concern about Nur al Din continued. He welcomed his long lost friend and spent time with him, patiently answering his questions, and praying for his salvation. Please pray for those who you'll meet today, tomorrow, and next week — you never know who God might send across your path. You might have only a short window of opportunity to influence their life for eternity.

1. How different could Nur al Din's life have been had he not rejected Nader's testimony?
2. What second chances has God sent your way?
3. Is there anyone in your life who could benefit from a second chance, even though he or she might not deserve it?

· ·

Reflections

_____

_____

_____

_____

_____

_____

_____

_____

_____

_____

_____

_____

_____

_____

_____

_____

_____

_____

_____

_____

23.

Two Families

Husbands, love your wives, just as Christ loved the church and gave Himself up for her.

Ephesians 5:25, NIV

Women in Iran face far-reaching discrimination under the law. They are denied equal rights in marriage, divorce, child custody, and inheritance. Evidence given by a woman in court is considered only worth half that given by a man. A girl under the age of thirteen can be forced to marry a much older man if her father permits it.

www.amnesty.org

<hr>

Rahim - Merciful

I'm from Iran. My wife's name is Amira. We came to Greece with our children not too long ago. This country is new to us. I was a successful businessman in Iran. My success caught the attention of the Iranian government. When the government offered a business partnership, naturally, I couldn't refuse.

Unfortunately, the government partnership wasn't successful. I experienced some very difficult financial challenges that resulted in bankruptcy.

Unfortunately, the government partnership wasn't successful. I experienced some very difficult financial challenges that resulted in bankruptcy. When the government issued a warrant for my arrest, I knew that the only option I had to keep my family safe was to flee the country.

When we arrived in Greece, Amira was pregnant with our second child. We had no money, no visa, and no permission to be in Greece. But she needed to go to the hospital. None of us spoke Greek, and we had no idea what to do. We were very discouraged. There were so many problems, but no solutions.

One day, I saw an Iranian political activist on the street in Athens. I knew he was working for the Nawrooz party. The man explained to me that their party was trying to help Iranians in countries outside of Iran, and asked how they could help us. I told him about the birth of our child and the related expenses that we were unable to pay. So this man actually found some money to help us with those financial needs. When he gave us the money to pay the hospital bill, he told me that we could find food and clothing from various Christian organizations that would help us.

We told the workers that we were looking for love and someone who would care.

We didn't wait long before we decided to visit Helping Hands. We found food and clothing for us and the children. We stayed for the Bible study and listened to the teacher speak about salvation and Jesus. It all made sense to both of us. After the class, we stayed a little longer and talked to one of the workers. He asked why we came, so I told him the truth. We were looking for love and someone who would care. We were looking for freedom. And then Amira told him that we needed someone to show us the way of peace and comfort for our hearts.

Everyone was very nice to us, so we decided to come on a regular basis. It didn't take us long to accept Jesus as our savior. Both of us wanted to follow Him. We felt we needed to share the truth about Him with others. I used to be a very angry person; I worked very hard, rarely spending time with my wife or son. When I finally got home at night, I was usually filled with the pressure and frustration of the business. Amira was often upset with me because I never had any desire to spend time with our son. She didn't understand how painful and difficult it was for me to relate to him, or to even communicate with him.

Jesus changed our lives. I can say that I sincerely love my children. Amira loves when I spend time with them and help her. We both know that it is all because of Jesus. It makes me happy to see my son smile. I know he tells others that his dad isn't the person he used to be — he is his friend now. Even Amira says I'm different. She says I treat her with love and respect.

We decided to continue to come to the Persian Christian Fellowship and to Helping Hands. Sometimes our friends tell us they have noticed the change, but we both praise God for this. It is only because of Jesus that I'm a different man now.

Not so long ago, Amira met Shada, a single Iranian mother with two boys and a girl. Her husband was a fanatic Muslim working for the government in Iran. Although she doesn't know exactly what he did, his work involved a lot of traveling. He had a chauffeur and spent a lot of time in government and army buildings. He also had four other wives that Shada didn't know about until just before she left Iran.

> *When her husband was home, he was very difficult to live*
> *with. Thankfully, he was gone most of the time on business*
> *or living with his other four wives.*

Shada told us of the abuse, beatings, and neglect toward her and the children. When her husband was home he was very difficult to live with. Thankfully he was gone most of the time on business or living with his other four wives.

When Shada arrived in Athens with her children, she found a job working in a shop. She was putting CD's into cases for one Euro ($1.50 in US dollars) per hour. She struggled to pay for shelter and food. The day they met, Amira invited her to Helping Hands.

When the staff met Shada, I think they saw the sadness in her eyes. They saw the same sadness in the eyes of her children. She has beautiful and polite children, but they distrust all men.

Amira and I kept telling Shada about what Jesus had done for our family. We always asked her to come with us when we went to Helping Hands.

The family kept coming with us and slowly Shada started to ask questions. Because she distrusted men, she had a hard time trusting Jesus. She greatly struggled with trusting any other man after how her husband acted.

But as she began to understand and believe that Jesus was not just a man, but God who loved her, she started to trust Him. Jesus became a loving Father, a friend to her. She accepted that Jesus was here to love her and to hug her, to heal her pain and give her peace.

Finally, Shada believed, and so did her fourteen-year-old daughter, sixteen-year-old son, and her youngest child; they all accepted Jesus. Today, she says that they found a friend who has cared for them and has given them peace when no other could.

• •

Rear-view Mirror

Our Father gives without reservations so that we can always pass His love, His compassion, His healing, and His forgiveness to others. We freely receive from His hand what is most valuable to us. We are never left empty-handed, and even in the midst of trouble, we can find a way to minister to others. This sacrificial giving of ourselves is the very thing that helps our own wounds to heal. Amira was a wounded wife, hurt by her husband's disrespect and rejection. Jesus performed a miracle in her life, and her husband is a new man now, who lives by the Word of God. He loves her and their children. He now understands that God created both men and women, and He created them both in His image, with equal value. When the couple met Shada, they saw the same deep wounds many women bear. Amira understood the depth of Shada's mistrust, but she also knew that there was only one person who could help her friend — Jesus. She not only identified with Shada's pain, but also shared the way to healing, and during that process, Amira's own soul healed too.

1. Why are women in most Muslim countries oppressed?
2. What are the differences and similarities between women's rights activism and the feminist movement?
3. Check around your community for what's being done for newcomers, especially women.

Reflections

24.

Loved

Still other seed fell on good soil. It came up and yielded a crop, a hundred times more than was sown.

Luke 8:8, NIV

Of particular concern to the UNHCR are Iranian refugees who entered Turkey from Iraq. These refugees have few prospects for durable solutions. Due to limited integration opportunities in Turkey, they face significant hardship. The UNHCR will continue to work with all its partners to find solutions for these refugees.

www.unhcr.org

Saquib – Shining Star

I'm twenty-eight years old, and I am from Tehran, Iran. I've lived outside Iran for almost seven years. I lived in Turkey for six years, and I have been in Greece now for almost seven months. Four years ago, I returned to Iran to get married, and then I returned to Turkey with my wife. After two years, God gave us our son, who is now eighteen months old. I gave him as a gift to God to use him anywhere. Because of the economic problems in Turkey, I sent my wife and son back to Iran nine months ago. I came to Greece by myself. I miss them every day.

I grew up in a strict Muslim house. When I was sixteen years old, I started work as a tailor in a shop that employed forty people. The owner of the shop was an Armenian Christian. One day he came to visit the shop. He came over to me. It was a Thursday, the last day of the Muslim week, when my week's work was already over. I was sewing a pair of trousers for myself. When he saw my work, he asked if I would like to work with him privately.

> When I told my parents, they didn't want to let me go. They believed my employer's family was unclean. They weren't Muslims. I shouldn't eat with them, and I shouldn't even accept their money.

Two weeks later, I quit the job at the shop and started working for him at his house. His house was far from our house, so my employer decided to let me sleep at his house. I would go home for the weekends. When I told my parents, they didn't want to let me go. They believed my employer's family was unclean. They weren't Muslims. I shouldn't eat with them, and I shouldn't even accept their money. But I told my parents that I knew them. They were really polite people, and I loved them.

My employer had two children. His son was four years younger than me, and his daughter was six years younger. We became like brothers and sisters. His wife loved me like her own child. She didn't let me wash my own clothes, but would do my laundry herself. I worked for them for five years. During that time, they talked about Jesus. My employer's wife was a wonderful believer. She wanted to make sure that I knew that Jesus was the Son of God, and that He is the only way to salvation.

> I was taught how to interrogate and brainwash people. There was even a mullah, an Islamic religious leader, who encouraged us to engage in Sighe, a sort of short marriage, blessed by a mullah.

When I got older, I had to go to the army. I became friends with my fellow soldiers and became more like them. I can say that before, when I was in my employer's house, I was not regularly involved in sinful activities. But during the two years I was with my fellow soldiers, I sinned enough to send me straight to hell. After a couple of months, I was reassigned to the religious police division. I was taught how to interrogate and brainwash people. There was even a mullah, an Islamic religious leader, who encouraged us to engage in Sighe, a sort of short marriage, blessed by a mullah. These marriages between a man and woman are set for a certain period of time, from two months to one year. The orphanages in Iran are mostly filled with children from these kinds of marriages. But after a couple of these Sighe marriages, something inside was bothering me. Questions kept coming back to me: don't you know anything about Jesus? Why are you doing this? I decided to walk separately from my friends. It was difficult because I was in the army.

When I got out of the army, I went to Turkey. I didn't know there was an Iranian church in Turkey. I'd never been to church. In Iran, my employer was afraid to bring me to a church; it would have been too dangerous. It's forbidden for Muslims to enter a church or for Christians to speak about their faith to Muslims.

> *They had heard us speaking Farsi. They gave us a book called*
> What Is Christianity? *Then they invited us to the church.*

After I had been in Turkey for four years, I was walking in the open-air market with my wife when I saw a man and a woman approaching us. They had heard us speaking Farsi. They gave us a book called *What Is Christianity?* Then they invited us to the church. I had talked to my wife prior to that about my employer and Christianity, and she was interested in Christianity, too. She didn't know anything about it but wanted to find out. We were so glad to find the church in Istanbul. During our first visit, we met Sister Gity from England; we were so impressed. After ten months, we saw the fruit of Jesus in our lives. We also saw a lot of miracles in our child's birth. So we decided to give our lives to Jesus and ask Him to live in us. We were baptized, and we asked Him to use us.

I want to share some of the things that have happened since we've believed in Jesus. Recently, my wife was sick. She was alone in Iran; we were apart because of the difficult refugee life in Greece. She was so depressed that she couldn't move half of her body. She couldn't sleep at all for a whole week. It was during the first Timothy Project, and Brother Themis asked us to all pray for each other. Brother Sam prayed for me. Two days later, when I came back to Athens from attending the Project, I called Iran. It was ten o'clock at night, and I woke her up! She told me that she had been able to sleep for two days now, from exactly the time that Sam prayed for her. I thank God for that.

I believe that all of our problems can be resolved by faith. I wish for all believers to refresh their spirits with faith and prayers. And I pray for unbelievers to open their hearts to have Jesus' love and peace inside. The grace of our God, Jesus Christ, be with you — forever.

• •

Rear-view Mirror

Purposeful acts of kindness, patient words, and silent prayers are all seeds sown by ordinary people, in faith. Sunday school teachers, nursery volunteers, youth leaders, soup kitchen helpers, prayer warriors, missionaries — every one of us is given daily opportunities to scatter around a little bit of faith seed. Over time, many of these grow, and although we may never see the harvest with our own eyes, we must trust that God will water, cultivate, and prune until the harvest comes. At times, our efforts might seem hopeless. Imagine how the wife of Saquib's employer would have felt if she had met Saquib in a uniform of the religious police, with a Sighe wife at his side. What would she have thought about all the prayers she had sent to God on behalf of this man? But how much would she rejoice today, knowing that the seeds sown on her knees didn't die, but God protected the seeds till the time they would spring to life. Saquib's troubles aren't over as he is still traveling along the refugee highway, but now, Jesus is traveling with him. Keep on spreading the seed. He is faithful to bring forth the harvest.

1. What role did the Christian family in Iran play in Saquib's life?
2. Think of a story of seed sown in good faith. What was the harvest?
3. Sow a seed. Sign off your e-mail with a note about refugees.

Reflections

_____

_____

_____

_____

_____

_____

_____

_____

_____

_____

_____

_____

_____

_____

_____

_____

_____

_____

_____

_____

25.

New Life

"It's a sad place. Hard to see how it can ever return to normal. No real joy, but there is the ability to survive. To move on, to try to rebuild. To try to make neighbours of old enemies."

Angelina Jolie
UNHCR Goodwill Ambassador
Journal on Kosovo, October 7, 2003

Gregor – The Artist

Gregor was an artist from Albania. When our team met Gregor for the first time, he was twenty-four years old. Through his very limited English and our non-existent Albanian, we soon understood that he was somewhat open to spiritual matters.

He accepted our invitation and watched the *Jesus* video in his mother tongue. When we sat down with him after the movie to see if he had any questions, it was obvious that he was very moved. He said that as a movie it was not so special, but as he watched it, he began to think. What if these things about Jesus are true? What if He is really like this? He told us about the intense internal battle he experienced while watching. His head was telling him one thing, but his heart was pulling in a different direction. At the end of the film, he had prayed the sinner's prayer and asked Jesus into his heart.

> *What if these things about Jesus are true? What if He is really like this?*

Although he had prayed during the movie, it was really about a week later, during a follow-up visit with short-term missionary named Tom, that Gregor clearly understood the message of the Gospel. A light had clicked on. From that day, Gregor had an insatiable hunger for God's Word. His passion and desire to do God's will was evident every time we met. He developed a consuming burden for the lost. Gregor had a meek and mild-mannered personality, but he has been gifted by the Holy Spirit with the gift of evangelism. We watched him grow in his faith and become instrumental in leading many other Albanians to the Lord.

While he was still in Athens, he led to the Lord his parents, a cousin, and a half-dozen friends in Albania through correspondence. As a result they, started a home fellowship in Gregor's home town of Shkoder, through which others came to the Lord. In Athens, Gregor was instrumental in leading several Albanians to the Lord, including his sister, brother-in-law, and his Muslim roommate.

Gregor's English quickly improved. He spent many hours in prayer, discipleship studies, and evangelism training. Before he had come to Christ, it had always been his dream to leave Albania and try to get to America, where he would be free to express his artistic gifts. However, now he began to sense that God was calling him to return as a witness to his fellow countrymen.

> *In October of 1992, Gregor returned to his home city, certain of God's calling on his life, but unclear about how to implement it.*

In October of 1992, Gregor returned to his home city, certain of God's calling on his life, but unclear about how to implement it. He later entered a YWAM discipleship training course (in cooperation with Frontiers) in Tirana that had a special emphasis on church-planting in Albania. Afterward, a team was formed. An outreach in Shkoder resulted in a church plant. The congregation continues to grow in impacting many in the area to this day. Gregor and the members of this new church initialized an evangelistic outreach to remote mountain villages in Albania, as well as to their own city. At the request of the government, and in cooperation with a few other churches, this group was also active during the Kosovar refugee crisis. They ran a transit center assisting three thousand refugees each day. This church also developed an outreach program to the refugees. Thousands of Kosovar refugees were touched by God's love through the church because of their care for their practical needs. Many were also awakened by the evangelistic and discipleship ministry in Albania. Some took Jesus back with them to Kosovo. Gregor's church started a relationship with a church in Kosovo that included special evangelistic teams from Shkoder, and the establishment of a one-year Bible school.

Some time after Gregor's parents came to the Lord, they entered a YWAM discipleship training course as well. They were both used to lead many people to the Lord. They also helped to plant the first church ever in a mountain city of fifteen thousand people previously unreached for Christ. One of the young men they led to Christ, Taulant, became a part of that church plant; he later joined Campus Crusade for Christ. As part of his ministry, he not only actively shared his faith with others, but also traveled around the country training others to share their faith as well.

Gregor and his wife, Kela, with their two young boys, moved to Kosovo in January of 2004 to begin a church-planting ministry there. They became part of a church-planting team and have worked hard with other missionaries in the area to bring Kosovars to Jesus. Along with their (now) three boys, they are praying about where they can go next to reach the unreached for Jesus.

• •

Rear-view Mirror

Desolation, displaced people, ruined economy — that was a picture of Kosovo that Angelina Jolie witnessed in 2003. But amidst this bleak situation, God was already at work. He had his people ready, sleeves rolled up, willing to give their all. God never gives up on his people. Like new seedlings after a massive forest fire, faith grows amidst ashes left by war. What difference can one person make? At times we tend to think we are insignificant in the greater framework of our world. We tend to wonder what we can do, watching headlines reporting on disasters, armed conflicts, or failing economies. Yet people like Gregor are a beacon of life. From watching a video to bringing Jesus to his nation during incredibly difficult times — as hundreds of thousands of refugees from Kosovo flooded into Albania — Gregor followed God's call. He was in the right place, at the right time, able to mobilize others and show the love of Jesus to thousands in the most practical way: the same way he and his family experienced the same love expressed to them, through the works and gifts offered by the missionary team in Athens. The ripple effect of what we can do with God's help is beyond our comprehension. God does work miracles with His most precious creation, His people — you. Thank you for partnering with Him.

1. What is your favorite part of this story? Why?
2. Read Mark, chapter five. What are the similarities in Gregor's story?
3. Find a basic need in your community — a homeless person, a food bank, or a clothing drop-off box. A small act of kindness goes a long way, so start your own ripple effect by meeting another's need today.

Reflections

_____

_____

_____

_____

_____

_____

_____

_____

_____

_____

_____

_____

_____

_____

_____

_____

_____

_____

26.

Seeker

At that time Jesus said, "I praise you, Father, Lord of heaven and earth, because you have hidden these things from the wise and learned, and revealed them to little children."

Matthew 11:25, NIV

Iran continues to sentence child offenders to death, despite signing international treaties that make this illegal. It was the only country to execute children in 2005. In 2006, it shares this position with Pakistan — the only other country to have executed a child so far this year.

www.amnesty.ca

Nafisa – Pure

I was born in Tehran as the only daughter of a very wealthy Iranian family. My father wasn't religious at all, and his scepticism rubbed off on me. I had to enroll in a private high school, attended mostly by Christian students, so that I wouldn't get in trouble at the public high school.

My Armenian Christian classmates would ask me questions about my official religion, but I couldn't answer, simply because I didn't know much about Islam. But I liked our discussions and wanted to learn more about Christianity. I even attended my friend's wedding just so I could see the inside of a church building.

She gave me a New Testament in Farsi, my native tongue.
When I asked about her later, no one in the area had seen
her or knew anything about her.

One day an American woman wandered into the expansive enclosure around our house.

I was surprised to see that anyone had managed to get by the four guards, not to mention the guard dogs that usually watched our gate. She was lost, so I walked her back to the street and pointed her in the direction of the address she was seeking. "Thank you," she said, "and, here, I have something for you." She gave me a New Testament in Farsi, my native tongue. When I asked about her later, no one in the area had seen her or knew anything about her.

The New Testament sat on a shelf in my room for a long time before I finally picked it up one night after another discussion about Christianity with my classmates. I began at the beginning of Matthew and read straight through. When I got to Mark, I realized that it was telling the same story, but I couldn't put it down. When I had finished John, it was four o'clock in the morning. This Jesus character fascinated me, and I wanted to learn all I could about Him.

I was stopped by the religious police, who searched my bag.
They found my books. Then they immediately arrested me.

One day, I telephoned my cousin and told her I wanted to talk to her about something interesting. I stuck into my bag my New Testament and a book criticizing Islam, which my friends at school had given me, and left for her house. Usually, I would take a cab when I went to see her, but this time I walked. I was stopped by the religious police, who searched my bag. They found my books. They immediately arrested me.

When my father found out, he went to the police station and talked to the guard on duty. "How much do you make in a year?" he asked the young soldier. The guard told him. "How about four times that amount right now?" The guard released me.

We had been to Greece before on family vacation, so it wasn't very difficult to get a tourist visa. My father signed documents that officially transferred his half of the factory and his business interests to my grandparents. My father, mother, and I got on a flight to Athens three days after I was arrested.

Life suddenly became very difficult. We lived with my uncle's family and worked in his restaurant. Three months after we first came to Athens, I realized I would never be able to return home. Around that time, my uncle cheated my father out of his money, and one of my cousins in Iran died. I was tired of living and tried to kill myself twice, but both times I was interrupted.

The day after my second suicide attempt, I passed by the First Greek Evangelical Church of Athens, saw the cross, and remembered why I had come to Athens in the first place.

The day after my second suicide attempt, I passed by the First Greek Evangelical Church of Athens, saw the cross, and remembered why I had come to Athens in the first place. I went home and announced that I would be attending church that Sunday. To my surprise, both of my parents said they would come with me. From that day, the three of us attended church every Sunday morning, starting with Sunday school at ten o'clock.

Even though I went to church every Sunday, I was still afraid to officially change my religion. Most of all, I was afraid of being the only Iranian that stopped being a Muslim and became a Christian. But one Sunday, I met an American woman who said that she knew a lot of Christian Iranians. I didn't believe her, but accepted her invitation to her English class at the Athens Refugee Center. The place was packed full of men, and I was scared, as I was the only woman there! Then the office door opened and one of the women who worked there asked if she could help me. She took me to the English class. I was surprised to see how many Iranians were there. After the lesson was over, the teacher introduced me to an Iranian who had converted from Islam to Christianity. I finally realized that I was free to listen to my heart.

When I got home, I prayed and said, "Okay, God, I've heard everything, now show me the truth. Which one is right? Show me who you really are." I fell asleep and had a dream. In my dream, someone told me: "I told you that I'm the Truth and the Life and the Way. No one comes to the Father except by me." I woke up and cried. I knew the truth. In the morning I called my pastor and asked how I could be baptized.

I continued coming to the English class at the Athens Refugee Center. Before my teacher returned to America, she asked if I would take over her class. In fact, I was getting very involved in volunteering at the ARC, despite telling myself I didn't need to go there anymore. Something inside me wouldn't let me stay away. It was there, working with other believers and seeing their example, that I discovered what it really meant to be a Christian.

I believe God has a call on my life to bring His truth to my people. I started doing that by translating, teaching English classes, and developing relationships with Iranians and Afghans here in Athens. Refugees are more open than Muslims living in their own homeland. I am currently serving refugees through my local church as a missionary with International Teams. God has brought into my life a godly husband and a new baby. One day, when the government finally changes, I want to return to Iran and tell my people about Jesus. If they could only read the Bible for themselves, I'm sure Iranians would see the truth about who God really is. He would show them the same way He has revealed Himself to me.

• •

Rear-view Mirror

Oppression and fear are the tools of darkness. When fundamental human rights are suppressed and there is no provision for justice, society crumbles. But our Heavenly Father doesn't manipulate us with fear. One of His greatest gifts to humankind was the gift of free will. He gave us the ability to choose good or evil. He also provided a way out of sin. As Nafisa's father paid a ransom for his daughter, our Heavenly Father paid a ransom for us. His only Son sacrificed Himself, so that we may have the freedom to choose what's right. In His death and resurrection, we have been reconciled to our Heavenly Father, who grants us full privileges as His children. We no longer live in fear because we know our Father will always come to our rescue. He doesn't promise life without challenges and troubles, but He promises never to leave us or forsake us. In the midst of darkness He is there with outstretched arms, offering hope. He knows our future, and He knows eternity, where there will be pain no more.

1. What do you think would have happened to Nafisa if her father had not been able to pay off the prison guard?
2. Recall a situation when someone came to your rescue. How did you feel about that person?
3. Pray that God will show you who needs to see a bit of God's light this week. Find a way to encourage him or her.

. . . .

Reflections

_____

_____

_____

_____

_____

_____

_____

_____

_____

_____

_____

_____

_____

_____

_____

_____

27.

Freedom

The Spirit of the Lord is on me, because He has anointed me to preach good news to the poor. He has sent me to proclaim freedom for the prisoners and recovery of sight for the blind, to release the oppressed.

Luke 4:18, NIV

There are 42 million forcefully displaced people in the world. That means that one person in every 161 on earth today has been forced from their homes and is in need of refuge.

UN, June 2009

Hamdan – Praiser of God

I knew about Christianity when I lived in Iran. I met a lot of Christians there, and they had many good characteristics that drew me to them. I saw a big difference between Christians and Muslims in their behavior, their speech, everything. I could easily tell if someone was a Christian or a Muslim. To me, the Christians acted like they had been in God's presence. But everyone knows that, in Iran, if you go to church or ask questions about Christianity, it's dangerous — you risk your life. There is no way to learn more.

When I left Iran, I wasn't escaping from any particular problem. I just wanted freedom. In Iran, there is no freedom; everything involves religion. Everyone has to keep their thoughts in their heads. There is no freedom of speech. If one speaks out, he or she is sure to get in a lot of trouble. The religious police stop everyone's mouth with religion.

> *I watched twelve- and thirteen-year-old boys, still children, beating the protestors without knowing why we were protesting. The only thing these boys knew was what they had been taught by their religious teachers.*

I remember the elections a few years ago. I attended a huge student demonstration in Tehran, and I saw the way the protestors were treated. I watched demonstrators being arrested. Many of them were never heard from again. I watched twelve- and thirteen-year-old boys, still children, beating the protestors without knowing why we were protesting. The only thing these boys knew was what they had been taught by their religious teachers. This is the way animals act, not good people.

So I left Iran for Turkey. When I had been there one month, I heard from Christian friends of mine back in Iran that there was an Iranian church in Istanbul. So I went. I was curious. I loved Christian people. I loved the way they talked. I loved the way they behaved. I wanted to be like them, but didn't care for their religion. I wanted to be like them but not one of them. I didn't want to change my religion. That would mean a lot of trouble for me.

> *He had to be absolutely certain about his faith in order to change his religion. I was shocked when he asked me if I wanted to change my clothes and be baptized too.*

Reza, one of my friends in Istanbul, told me he wanted to go to church one Sunday and asked if I would go with him. I told him I would. It happened to be a baptism day, but my friend didn't tell me that. At this church, the baptismal candidates wore white robes. There was a special ceremony, and all of them got baptized inside the church building. I was Muslim, and my friend had been Muslim. It was a sin for a Muslim to do this. But it was also a huge testimony to me. He had to be absolutely certain about his faith in order to change his religion. I was shocked when he asked me if I wanted to change my clothes and be baptized, too.

I told him I thought he was homesick and alone, and that's why he had changed his religion. I thought it was only because the church people were nice to him and accepted him. I was very angry with him. But he didn't listen to me. I was sad that he was so lost.

When the congregation sang, the worship songs were printed out on sheets of paper, and I followed along with the words, but the paper shook because my hands were trembling. I loved the way the people prayed with joy instead of weeping. They danced for their God instead of flaying themselves until they bled, like some Muslims do. I wanted to be able to pray to God with joy, too, not with sadness.

I stayed until the end of the service, but I was sad. Even so, the next week I told my friend I would go to church with him again. I secretly decided that if my questions would get answered that day, only then I would come again the following week. I went to the church for five months, every week. I became a regular. I also decided to attend Bible studies. In the Bible class, I was told by the teacher that if I wanted to say anything about the Koran, I would have to bring him a translation, so that he could read it for himself. If I wanted to say anything about the Bible, he asked me to do the same, bring a translation with the verses I quoted from.

Later, Mahmud, another student in the class, told me that I should first think about my questions, and see if I can figure them out by myself, look for the answers myself before I ask the teacher. I tried it. As I read Genesis, I would ask a question in my head, and the answer would suddenly occur to me. As time went on, I could answer my own questions, as if something were pushing or helping me along the way.

Whenever we had class, I would always sit in a place where no one could see me from the street, but Mahmud told me that people would eventually find out that I attended the Bible classes and treat me badly. My roommates did wonder where I went three times a week. They asked why I would leave the house well dressed, even on my day off. The only time I wouldn't invite them to come with me was when I went to the church.

> *After the service, I knew that, if I went home, my roommates and friends would not treat me the same ever again. I was afraid that they would do something terrible to me.*

Our house was rented in my name and another man's name, but other people lived there, too. One day, my roommates followed me on my way to church. One of my best friends came into the church and saw me there. He sat next to me and said he felt sorry for me. After the service, I knew that, if I went home, my roommates and friends would not treat me the same ever again. I was afraid that they would do something terrible to me.

I did go home that night. When I got there, I found by best friend sleeping under a blanket he had given to me some time ago. He left a note on my bed: "I'm sorry that it's cold, but I can't do anything about it." The next day my roommates teased me unmercifully. The house became a prison for me. I had rented the house in my name and invited them to move in, but now I wanted to leave it. But I also wanted to help them. God was working in me. Slowly, He brought me to forgive my best friend and other old roommates for their attitude and behavior. They tried their best to make me angry and leave, but I think God gave me the power to treat them with love in exchange for their ridicule.

Reza, my friend who first brought me to church, planned to go to Greece. I had tried unsuccessfully to go to Greece three or four times. I didn't want to live in Turkey. I wanted to live in a better country, a land where I could legally work. One day I saw Reza, and he told me that he had found a new way to get to Greece: by the sea. We bought an inflatable raft that was so cheap you could poke a hole in it with your finger. Nevertheless, we were determined to paddle across the Mediterranean in it.

We put the raft in the water and immediately lost one of the oars. I said, "We have to go back." I was scared. Reza told me not to worry; God would help us. "It's one in the morning. It's impossible," I answered. But in five minutes, we had found the missing oar.

I was afraid because the weather was windy and the waves were too big. I yelled at Reza, "I want to live!" But Reza encouraged me to keep paddling. We were in the sea for four and a half hours. We tried to get closer to our destination, but the wind just blew us back. Our arms were tired, we couldn't row anymore, but we called on God to help us. Suddenly, twenty meters away, a big ship was coming toward us. I said, "Okay, now we will die, because the ship is coming toward us, and we don't have any more strength to paddle away." Instead, the ship missed us by five meters, but the people on board didn't see us, and we didn't get caught in the wake. We prayed, and God had helped us. We paddled with our feet and hands and finally got to Greece at six in the morning.

After this experience, I decided to get baptized. We heard that there was a church in Greece that could do it. I told Reza that getting baptized was my new goal. When I arrived in Athens, I found a friend who told me about a Christian place called Helping Hands. We came together to attend the Baptism classes. I even translated for the teacher. I was finally baptized with water one day at a nearby beach, and was baptized with the Holy Spirit the same day.

My life has changed very much since I've become a Christian, my behavior, my speech, my attitude toward other human beings, the ability to feel their problems. When I got baptized I felt clean, and I was very happy. I try not to have sin in my life anymore. I ask God to guide me. I don't know what the future holds, but I hope that I will be able to start a new life in a new place. I live in one of Helping Hands' Nests. Even so, in Greece, I have many problems. I hate being called a refugee. It is very difficult to find work, and even more difficult to leave for another European country. But at least I'm free, politically and spiritually.

. . . .

Rear-view Mirror

Lost at sea, in the dark, without a sense of direction, without a compass. Imagine the intense fear these men experienced, with waves crashing against the small inflatable boat, and strong winds threatening to capsize it. Yet they chose to pursue their dreams. How often do the circumstances around us seem impossible, threatening our existence? How often are we tempted to throw in the towel and quit? Yet, we decide to swim against the current and pursue our dream. We might even ask ourselves in the midst of turmoil, why have we stepped out on such a path in the first place. What propels us to reach for new heights, take on new projects, and try what hasn't been tried before? Some call it a spirit of adventure; others might say it is pure craziness. But what if God Himself implanted this strong drive in us? What if this need to explore and search is a gift? Is it possible that this need to progress is pre-programmed in our DNA? Think of it, could God place a want in our souls? An empty space that only He can fulfill? Many of us search all our lives to fill that void. We try work, family, love, possessions, food, some turn to alcohol and drugs —we all are driven to find that one thing that will satisfy this perpetual thirst.

Jesus offers us what no one else can, "Whoever drinks the water I give him will never thirst." Could this mean that in finding Him, we will also find our purpose in life? Jesus continues, "The water I give him will become in him a spring of water welling up to eternal life" (John 4:14, NIV). Is it possible that the true purpose of our being will not only quench the thirst in this life, but carry on to eternity? As Christians, we believe that life has a meaning. Now it's our turn to find out what that meaning is for each one of us.

1. What gave these two men the strength to overcome their fear?
2. Recall a situation when you had to step out of your comfort zone and press through fear to accomplish something that you had never done before.
3. Pray that God will clearly show you your purpose in life. Ask Him to help you overcome the fear that could stop you from pursuing His vision for your life.

Reflections

_____
_____
_____
_____
_____
_____
_____
_____
_____
_____
_____
_____
_____
_____
_____
_____
_____
_____
_____

28.

The Treasure

The kingdom of heaven is like treasure hidden in a field. When a man found it, he hid it again, and then in his joy went and sold all he had and bought that field.

Mathew 13:44, NIV

Do not wait for leaders; do it alone, person to person.

Mother Teresa

ElhAm – Revelation

I was born in Iran, into a family that didn't believe in Islam. Like all Muslim girls, I learned about religion at school through the mandatory classes. As I grew up and started to read books outside of class, I realized that there were many contradictions among verses in the Koran. I started to seek and read more books to find out the truth.

> *I also took courses in history, from the time of Mohammad until now. I wanted to know that what I was taught was the same faith Mohammad taught.*

I read that Mohammad believed that politics and religion should be kept separate. But in the Koran, we see that they always go together. Our country is a religious country. The religious leaders think that they are doing things exactly as they were done in Mohammad's day. Because of that, I decided to go to the university and study political science, and I also took courses in history, from the time of Mohammad until now. I wanted to know that what I was taught was the same faith Mohammad taught.

While I was still in the university, I went to work for a newspaper. I met a Christian woman at work who talked to me about her religion. Our boss heard us talking and became very angry. He knew that I was a Muslim and that she was Christian.

He was afraid that she would try to convert me, which is illegal in Iran. He warned me not to talk to her any more, or I would be fired. I was afraid to talk to her. But during the short amount of time I spent with her, I could tell that she was a good woman. She was faithful, kind, and peaceful. I started to wonder about the differences between our religions, because while she was peaceful, we were always nervous and fearful. One day, the boss told her to leave. I had no opportunity to talk to anyone about Christianity, but I always wanted to know about the differences.

After I got married, my husband and I had to leave Iran. We went to Holland and stayed at a Christian youth hostel. As we checked in to the hostel, the staff gave us a book of the gospel of John, called *Living Water.* I didn't have anything else to do, so I started to read it. I opened up the book and read that Jesus was the light. In the evenings, there was a Bible discussion at the hostel. Someone came to my husband and me that first day, and invited us to the Bible study. My husband couldn't understand because he didn't speak English. But we went.

The question that day was: Who is God? There were about five of us there, and Nathan, the leader, didn't know that we weren't Christians. He asked me who I thought Jesus is. I said that Jesus is the light. The discussion continued. At the end people stayed and asked my husband and me questions. They knew we were from Iran, so they asked what our religion was. I answered, Islam, but in name only. That was the beginning of our daily Bible discussions.

> *As I read through the Gospels, more and more questions came to my mind. Each day I went to the staff at the hostel to ask them my questions.*

I asked the staff of the hostel for a Bible, but they didn't have any Farsi Bibles. I took an English Bible, but it was too difficult for me to read.

They gave me a dictionary, but it was still too hard to read. I found a Turkish Bible, but that was difficult as well. Then the staff decided to pray for a Farsi Bible for me. They prayed, and after two days they found one stuck between two stacks of books at another shelter run by the same organization. I was so happy. I could read it in my own language and understand more.

As I read through the Gospels, more and more questions came to my mind. Each day I went to the staff at the hostel to ask them my questions. I also attended church each Sunday.

One day, the manager of the hostel came to me and said that he found an Iranian church in another city, and asked if we would like to go. The next Sunday, one of the hostel staff members and I were supposed to go to that church, but there was a big storm, so we had to turn around and come back. I was very upset, but the manager told me that I could get a ride to the church again the next Sunday. I was really excited. The following Sunday, two staff members and I went to the service where I met some Iranian Christians. I was so glad, because they gave me the answers to my questions in my own language. It made such a difference to me. I could fully understand the deep meaning of what they said. I can't express how much it meant to me to hear the songs they sang about Jesus in Farsi. I had never heard anything like that, nor had I ever seen people praying like that in my language before. It was like Jesus was standing right in front of them, and they were talking face to face.

When we came back from church, I went to talk to one of the staff. I asked her what a person who wants to become a Christian needs to do. She told me that all you need to do is trust in Jesus as your Savior, to know that He died because of us. I told her that I did believe, and she asked me if I wanted her to pray with me. She prayed that I would be closer to God, and that He would touch my heart. She told God that she knew there was a party in heaven right now because I became a believer. She told me that I was now her sister. I told her that I didn't believe in God before He brought me here. It was His plan for my life to come to Him and serve Him.

Two days later, someone stole all of our luggage. I cried. The staff was very kind to me. I said that perhaps God is trying to see whether I believe or not. But they answered that this wasn't from God, because God didn't want to make me unhappy. It was from Satan, because he knew we're with

God now, and he wanted to attack us. A week later, we were robbed again. This time I didn't cry. It just made me go closer to God.

> *The pastor talked to me and said that I may face many problems because Muslims aren't allowed to change their religion. I told him that I believed that, if someone wanted something precious, they would have to pay its price.*

A man from the Iranian church told me that I needed to be baptized as a symbol of the death of my old life and the beginning of my new life. Then I found out that I had to leave Holland and go to Greece. But because I found Jesus in Holland, I wanted to be baptized in that country, surrounded by all my friends who told me about Him and led me to Him. I only had five days before I had to leave. I asked the manager of the hostel if she could arrange for me to be baptized before I left. We had to leave on Wednesday morning, but she was able to arrange everything so that I could be baptized on Tuesday. The only thing I had to do was to talk to the pastor of the Iranian Church.

On Sunday, one of the staff members and I went to the church. The pastor talked to me and said that I may face many problems because Muslims aren't allowed to change their religion. I told him that I believed that if someone wanted something precious, they would have to pay its price. I was prepared to do that. He accepted my answer and agreed to baptize me. When the other staff heard about it, they were very happy. When I saw that, I decided to get baptized right there, so that they could celebrate with me. I was baptized that afternoon by the pastor of Christ Church. After that, my friends at the hostel and I celebrated all evening.

When we came to Greece, we had many problems. But I prayed and knew that God would take care of us. A few days later, I met an Iranian Christian girl at a church. She helped us a lot. I'm so grateful to God that He made me part of His family, and that even though I'm here without my own family, I know that I'm part of His and He is taking care of me. I would like to tell all the staff at the youth hostel how grateful I am. I'm a changed person, and I owe all that I am now to them. They were the ones who told me about Jesus. Thank you so much for all you have done for me.

. . . .

Rear-view Mirror

The Kingdom of God is like a hidden treasure. At times it might not seem that way to us, as we live our Christian lives in freedom and democracy. We can pray to God anytime we like, we can openly read the Bible, and we are able to go to church every Sunday. But what about our brothers and sisters around the world? Some have to worship in secret, read only when others are fast asleep, or sneak away to secret gatherings. They risk their relationships, families, security, and often lives to share their faith. Only the Lord knows how many have been punished, rejected or even put to death by their families or governments, because they chose to follow Him. Let us remember their courage and determination. Please pray for those who suffer because of their Christian faith. Pray for their strength, pray for their rescue, pray that their captors will be changed by the witness of these suffering believers. Our God is merciful and kind, please pray for His mercy and kindness to shine today on those who are imprisoned, hurt or ridiculed because they chose Jesus as their Lord.

1. What obstacles could ElhAm face for becoming a Christian? What did she mean when she said there is a price to pay?
2. What opposition have you faced as a believer?
3. Visit www.persecution.net. Pray as the Lord leads you.

Reflections

29.

The Door

Every Scripture is God-breathed and profitable for instruction, for reproof and conviction of sin, for correction of error and discipline in obedience, [and] for training in righteousness, so the man of God may be complete and proficient, well fitted and thoroughly equipped for every work.

II Timothy 3:16-17, AMP

In Asia and Pacific regions, the total refugee population increased by 1 million due to the inclusion of 1.1 million Afghans in a refugee-like situation. Refugee figures for Pakistan include recognized Afghan refugees (1,700), registered Afghans in refugee villages who are assisted by the UNHCR (886,700), and registered Afghans outside refugee villages who are living in a "refugee-like" situation (1,147,800).

2007 UNHCR Statistical Yearbook

Armagan – Gift

As a young man in Afghanistan, I had heard of Jesus. Like other Muslims, I thought He was a special prophet. I respected Him and even believed that He rose from the dead, but I didn't believe that He was God.

It all started with a dream about Jesus. I'd been thinking about my future. I told my parents that I wanted to change my religion and leave Afghanistan. At first, they were very upset and angry, and for a while they thought I was insane. I had been a very religious Muslim all my life. In the end, my parents' love for me was stronger than their anger, and they did not forbid my pursuits.

> *I dreamed that I had left Afghanistan and become a Christian.*
> *I dreamed that I had been baptized in a sea.*

A while later, I had a second dream; I dreamed that I had left Afghanistan and become a Christian. I dreamed that I had been baptized in a sea.

When I was seventeen years old, I rejected Islam and began searching for the truth. My friends didn't understand; some were convinced that I had become an atheist. But Afghanistan was not a place for religious experimentation. I knew that if I wanted to learn more about Jesus, I would need to leave. My sister's husband suggested that I learn English. My parents, who had never learned to read their own language, cheered me on.

As I studied, something wonderful happened: I met an American family of Christians in Afghanistan. They welcomed me like a son. They were honest, gracious, and full of hope. I could see that their lives were different, and I was attracted to their optimism. I wondered how I could find the same joy. I had a strange feeling, as if there were a hidden door through which I could walk to begin a new life. I didn't know how to find that door, but I felt that these Christians were closer to it than anyone I'd ever met before.

> *I loved that family and wanted to become like them. I thought*
> *that I could do this by going to America.*

I loved that family and wanted to become like them. I thought that I could do this by going to America. I asked the mother how I might accomplish this. "It isn't easy", she said, "but if God wants you to go to America, He'll lead you there."

So my journey began. From Afghanistan, I went to Pakistan, and then on to Iran. There, my curiosity about Jesus grew. How could I find out more about this forbidden faith? I found my answer in an unlikely place: on the street. As I wandered in the markets, I saw a vendor selling Bibles. I bought one and marveled that I hadn't been caught, since buying Bibles is illegal for Muslims in Iran.

First, I read the Old Testament, then the New Testament. Much of what I read mystified me. I tried to attend a Christian church in Iran, but the Christians learned that I was a Muslim and wouldn't let me enter the building. They were afraid. Also in Iran, I saw a movie that claimed that Jesus was the Son of God and that He died on the cross to pay the price for the sins of the world. Later in Turkey, I went to Catholic and Orthodox churches and learned a bit more. When I arrived in Athens, I slept in Alexandras Park for two months. Then someone there told me about Helping Hands in Omonia. At Helping Hands, I ate soup and met other guys my age who were traveling west. I went to the English and Bible lessons.

I liked the friendly Christians who ran the center. I especially liked the Bible teacher. He told us that Jesus could give a person a new life. He read from the Injil, the New Testament, "When someone becomes a Christian he becomes a new person inside." I always thought that going to America might give me a better life, but our teacher suggested that knowing Jesus would give me the best life, no matter where I was.

But that wasn't the answer I wanted to hear. I joined a group of men who planned to go to Italy. As we waited for the ferry boat in Patras, a woman approached me and handed me a book about Jesus. I was stunned. There are hundreds of people here in the crowd. Why did she give this book to me? Meanwhile, passengers were boarding the ferry boat and my friends urged me to follow them. But I realized that I didn't want to follow them, and felt an urge to return to Athens.

> *The Bible teacher listened patiently and then asked me why I wanted to change my religion. "Do you want to become a Christian to go to America, or to know Jesus?" he asked. That was a hard question because I wasn't sure.*

When I got back to Omonia, I marched into Helping Hands. I told the Bible teacher about the woman in Patras and said that I wanted to become a Christian. The Bible teacher listened patiently and then asked me why I wanted to change my religion. "Do you want to become a Christian to go to America, or to know Jesus?" he asked. That was a hard question because I wasn't sure. I thought about it and realized that my motives were mixed. I asked God to show me which religion I should choose. I prayed that God would show me the way. Then I had a third dream: I dreamt of the cross, and I heard Jesus say, "I am the way, the Truth, and the Life. No one comes to the Father, but through me."

Shortly after that, the Bible teacher asked me to translate some of the Koran into English. As I read the passage describing Jesus' birth, I compared the Koran's account with the Injil's, and was convinced that Jesus wasn't only a prophet, but the Son of God who came to earth to die for my sins and to give me a new life. That exact moment was the important encounter that awaited me in Athens, the most important encounter of my life. Soon I was baptized in the sea — my boyhood dream became real.

What have I gained from following Jesus? First, I have joy. I'm very happy because I know that Jesus has saved me from my sins. I'm also happy because, through Jesus, I can know God and can talk to Him like a son talks to his father. God also encourages me during the hard times when the realities of the world bring me pain. Last year, for example, I had a bad accident in Athens and I was tempted to doubt God. But I learned that suffering builds my faith.

Trusting Jesus as my Savior has also helped my attitude. Before I was a Christian, I was a good, hard worker who minded the law. But I was also very proud and I judged other people harshly. Now I'm humbled that Jesus took the punishment for my sins, and I know that I am only saved by His grace. God has given me love for my enemies, patience, and the peace that my life is safe in His hands.

One of my favorite stories in the Injil is the story of Jesus and the demon-possessed man who lived among the tombs. The man was hopeless. But Jesus healed him and gave him a new life. Before He left the man, Jesus told him to return to his house and describe what great things God has done for him. The man went away, proclaiming throughout the whole city what great things Jesus had done for him. I feel like that man. Jesus has given me a new life, and He can give you a new life, too.

As you read this, I am somewhere in Italy, or perhaps I am even further in my journey. I don't know if I'll ever see America, but that isn't as important to me now. I have found the Door to a new life, and His name is Jesus.

Rear-view Mirror

Do you ever think back to the time when you first found your faith? Were you born into a Christian family, living the Christian life since childhood? Did you always know in your heart that there was a God somewhere out there, or was the good news of Jesus something unexpected? Many of us were raised without faith. We might have been atheists, or perhaps just indifferent to any kind of spiritual life. But as we mature from childhood to adulthood and start looking for our own voice, our own place in this world, our mind floods with questions. Is all that our parents told us true? How is all that I have learned so far reflected in my life? Am I happy with who I am? Am I content with my life? Is there something more? Family, friends, career, money, and influence are wonderful things to have in our lives, but none of these make us complete. The day we ask for the first time if there is something more out there, we acknowledge the deep need for God. We embark on a quest to find what that "something more" is. At times, it is a conscious search, but often we wander from thing to thing, project to project, accomplishment to accomplishment and don't understand why we don't feel fulfilled and happy. Nothing can take His place. We are created with a built-in homing device, which is set to find Him. Only in Him we find our true purpose, our gifting, our mission in life, and only in Him will we feel fulfilled. He is our Alpha and Omega, beginning and end.

He created us, gave us life, equipped us for life in this world, during this particular time in history, and made us an irreplaceable part of it. It is only up to us to search for His wisdom and find out what role we are to play. There are no accidents with God, He knows you, He knows the purpose He gave you, and He knows your heart. Pray for courage to embrace His plan for your life.

1. What did Armagan learn from his Bible teacher?
2. How did God fulfill your search for meaning in your life?
3. Visit www.refugeeweek.org.uk/simple-acts and pick yours for today.

Reflections

_____

_____

_____

_____

_____

_____

_____

_____

_____

_____

_____

_____

_____

_____

_____

_____

_____

_____

30.

Hope for the Future

Herald and preach the Word! Keep your sense of urgency, whether the opportunity seems to be favorable or not.

II Timothy 4:2, The Amplified Bible

The Taliban's growth in much of Afghanistan's south and east is far less about ideology than jobs. There are legions of unemployed young men over there, and they're never going to get married and start a family if they don't have a job, so when the Taliban comes by and offers them ten US dollars a day to lay roadside bombs or participate in ambushes, a lot of them sign up.

Rajiv Chandrasekaran Washington Post Associate Editor

Navid – Reward

I was born into one of the most politically powerful tribes in Afghanistan. My grandfather was a good friend of the king and was himself the governor of northern Afghanistan. My grandfather's highest hope for my father as he was growing up was that he continue the family tradition of political and religious leadership. But my father wasn't very interested in religion, and he felt honored when he was one of a few students handpicked to be trained at the prestigious army university. His decision to join the army upset the entire family, but on the day he was to start at the university, my grandfather died, so no one in the family could oppose him.

After he had been at the university for two years, the Soviet army chose some people to go to Russia for more military education. My father and all his classmates were transferred to flight school to become pilots. After finishing his education, my father returned to Afghanistan and married my mother. My mother was the daughter of one of the most powerful people in the government at that time.

> *One of my dad's best friends was killed in the revolution, and to honor his memory, my father named me after him when I was born later that year.*

Soon after my parents' marriage, Russia gained more influence in the government and decided to put the people they had trained into positions of power. My father was made the commander of the first military airport. In April of 1978, he and many of the others who trained in Russia started a successful Communist revolution and took over the government. One of my dad's best friends was killed in the revolution, and to honor his memory, my father named me after him when I was born later that year. Two years later, my brother was born, and my dad chose a name for him from another of his fallen friends.

A while after, another Communist movement started, and my father was put under house arrest for two years. After the two years, my family was moved to Kandahar because another political faction wanted to use my father as a political symbol. They gave him a job, but no real power.

Yet another revolution occurred, and the new group in power sent my dad to study in Russia again. They were afraid to have him in the country because they thought he might try to overthrow them. He studied political science at Lenin University in Moscow. The first year he was in Russia, one of his friends was called back to Afghanistan and killed by the government. My youngest brother was named after that friend. During the year that he was in Russia without us, my father worried that we were in danger. My mother was afraid, too, so she kept me at home and taught me herself rather than sending me to school where I could be harmed. In 1985, my father asked us to join him in Russia where we would be safer. I started school there in Moscow.

In 1990, my family moved back to Afghanistan. Again my dad gained power in a political group, and he became a leader of the air force. He became a leader of the Defense Ministry. One of the mujahedeen, the group that later became the Taliban, wrote to my father and asked him to work with them to change the government. He refused their offer.

The mujahedeen successfully took over the country, and most of the people who had been in power previously ran away from Afghanistan. Because my dad was from one of the most respected tribes in Afghanistan, he returned to his home city, hoping that fear of his family and tribe would keep others from harming him. He feared that he would be a target, but remained confident that no one would want to defy his family.

When I was thirteen years old, I went to stay with my grandparents for a month. I loved to visit my mother's parents, who lived about one hundred kilometers away. After I had only been there for two days, someone came to take me back to my parents' house. I was angry that my vacation was interrupted and didn't want to go. When I arrived home, I saw a huge crowd gathered around my house. I saw my uncles and thought, "Why are they here?"

> *I had been brought home to attend the funeral for my entire family. I learned that people had gathered in front of my house at night and killed everyone inside — my father, my mother, and my two little brothers.*

My memories from that day are the worst, saddest pictures of my life. I had been brought home to attend the funeral for my entire family. I learned that people had gathered in front of my house at night and killed everyone inside — my father, my mother, and my two little brothers. Worst of all, my mom was pregnant. My parents had desperately wanted to have a daughter and hoped that this one would be a girl.

I wouldn't talk to anyone. My grief made me crazy. I was sent back to my grandparents' home, and from that day, my grandmother and grandfather became my parents. Since I was the only one in my family left alive, my uncle was afraid that I was in danger. He took me to Kabul so that I would be safe.

In 1992, the situation in Afghanistan grew even worse, so I went with a younger friend to Tashkent, the capital of Uzbekistan. I started studying martial arts, and as my love for them grew, so grew my hatred for others.

I thought that if I grew stronger and more powerful in the martial arts, I could kill whomever I wanted to. The son of one of the previous leaders of Afghanistan founded the school I attended in Uzbekistan, hoping to train people who would one day go back and retake power. He encouraged me in my hatred and told me that one day I would be powerful and could punish the people who had killed my family. I waited for the day when I could finally take power and have my revenge.

After a year, the economy in Uzbekistan worsened, so I moved back to Afghanistan. I went to Kabul and dedicated myself to school, knowing that education would help me gain power. In 1995, I joined the Youth Islamic Group, even though I was not a Muslim. I was the only one who was brave enough to speak in front of people, so I started being given leadership roles. In my last year of high school, I became a vice president of the group. I started reading the Koran and other books about Islam, and daily became more interested in learning about the faith. The former king hoped that the Youth Islamic Group would one day take over the government. The group chose several students to go to university in Egypt, and I was among those selected. They sent me to Pakistan first, and there I was rejected for the university because I was not a member of a Pashtu party. They saw my past and rejected me. This time in Pakistan was very difficult for me.

When I went back to Afghanistan, the Taliban was gaining strength. I went to Mazar-e-Sharif and registered for law school. The political situation got even worse, so I went to Iran. I sold two of the houses that my family owned and started a company importing rice from Pakistan. For five years, I had a great life in Iran. I connected with the previous government of Afghanistan through the embassy in Iran. With their help, I opened an office of the Islamic Youth Group.

I read a great deal, studying the lives of strong leaders who threw off their oppressors. I loved reading about Hitler, Nelson Mandela, Napoleon Bonaparte, and Patrice LeMumba. I began to idolize Adolf Hitler. My vision was to become like him, to achieve what he achieved. I learned everything I could about him — I could probably write a book on Hitler, I know so much about him. I think I didn't even love my father or my best friend as much as I loved Hitler. I wouldn't smoke, drink alcohol, or have relations with any woman because I wanted to be like him.

When America entered Afghanistan after the attacks of September 11, 2001, all the Afghans living outside the country were filled with hope. I went back to Afghanistan thinking that we would finally have democracy. I thought that with everything happening now, I could really take power. I thought it was a great opportunity for Afghanistan. But quickly I saw that there was no real change. Everything stayed the same; they just substituted one person's name for another. Everyone who had power before still retained their power. The man who killed my family is the leader of the military in north Afghanistan — he has more power now than ever before. My uncle warned me that my existence was a threat to that man and that he would try to kill me because he knew I would stand against him. So I left again, and went back to Iran for two months.

My relatives in England encouraged me to come to Europe. They paid a smuggler to take me to Turkey. We walked from Tehran to Istanbul, over the mountains, for nine days.

In the room where I was staying with a friend, I found an old and torn-apart book. It was the Gospel of Matthew. I read it not because I was interested in it, but because it was the only thing I could find to read in Farsi, and I really missed reading. A few things in the book caught my attention. I read that if anyone slaps your face, you should turn the other cheek. I also read, "Let your 'Yes' be 'Yes,' and your 'No,' 'No.'" Muslims are always swearing that they will do something, but then they don't. The more I read, the more I realized that even though Muslims view Jesus as a prophet, the teachings in the Koran are exactly opposite to what he taught.

After staying in Turkey for a month-and-a-half, I paid a smuggler about 2,500 dollars to take me to Greece. When I arrived in Athens, I only had one phone number, and the person I called took me to the "Afghan Hotel," an apartment filled with Afghan refugees. I was just planning to stay for as long as it took for my family to find someone to smuggle me to Belgium and then on to Germany. While I was waiting, I talked to an Iranian man named Hamid, who also lived in the hotel. I asked him if he would take me to a church. He said, "I will show you, but I will never, never enter that place."

I came to Helping Hands in the afternoon, and the only person there was Mohammed. From the way that he greeted me and talked with me, I felt like he had known me for ages.

I came to Helping Hands in the afternoon, and the only person there was Mohammed. From the way that he greeted me and talked with me, I felt like he had known me for ages. He was friendly, and it was really touching. After I had come to Helping Hands several times, Mohammed gave me a Farsi New Testament and Josh McDowell's *More Than a Carpenter*.

I knew a lot about Islam and the Koran from studying so much and from leading the Islamic group. I believe that Islam is about killing and hatred. Many times in Afghanistan I saw people killed and mutilated in the name of God. When I saw the difference between the two religions, I accepted Christ. I had missed my family for a long time, and when I was around Christians I felt that I was part of a family again. The Christians I met were so open and loving that I felt like I belonged, and I needed that.

My relatives sent a smuggler to take me to Germany, but I didn't want to go with him. I knew my family wouldn't be happy that I became a Christian. I knew they would try to change me. I decided to stay in Athens so that I could study more about the Bible. As my heart grew stronger in faith, I realized that I had never felt so good and that I needed to learn more about God. I thought about this great gift of peace I had received, and I needed to share this peace with others. I knew that if all the Afghan people would feel like I felt, there would be no more war. All the fighting would end. That was when I decided I would stay, study more, grow stronger, and then return to Afghanistan instead of going on to another country.

There have been many big changes in my life since I invited Jesus into it, and I am free from the bondage of sin. I feel like I am not alone any more, and I don't long for my family like I used to. I used to do whatever I wanted to do, but now I know that there is a person that I can trust holding my hand, and He will help me walk in the places that He wants me to go. I have also forgiven the people who killed my family. I hold nothing against them now.

I feel a lot of responsibility toward my people in Afghanistan, and I want to give them the things that I have found. My country has been at war for twenty-five years. Thousands and thousands of people have been born into war and have grown up in war, and that's all they know in life. The only thing they know is hatred. I was one of those people, but now I have found love. I believe that for Afghanistan there can only be one solution, only one doctor that can help the country — and that is Jesus Christ. No one else could take away the hatred that fills the land.

My vision is to gather a group of believers unified by the same goal and return to Afghanistan together. We can spread out to different cities, reaching more places for Christ in the country at the same time. I plan to build a church and an orphanage on the family property that I still have in Afghanistan. I want to give all my life, until the last moment that I am here, for God.

If my story has touched you, please pray for Afghanistan. Pray also that God will continue to grow my heart. Pray that the things He has planted there will grow deeper and deeper, stronger and stronger.

• •

Rear-view Mirror

Whom does the Lord choose? The weak? The strong? The Lord makes no such choice. He calls to Himself all His children. We all are created in His image, regardless the language we speak or the passport we hold. We all face the same call and the responsibility for our choice. The Lord can do miracles, yet He will not force us to participate. We have to decide of our own free will to follow, to obey, and to do the work of His Kingdom. On the pages of this book you have met a number of people, faced with difficult and often tragic circumstances. Many of them are homeless, stateless, and unwanted even today. The UN statistics are overwhelming, but apathy must not be our default response to this worldwide crisis. There are millions of needy people scattered across our planet, and each one of us holds the key to change. Most of us lack political influence or large sums of money to make a dramatic change in lives of the masses, but each of us can do something, just like the boy with a few fish and some bread. When we offer what we have in faith to our Master, He can receive it, bless it and turn it into a miracle. The purpose of this book is to encourage you to pray and ask Him to show you the way toward change.

1. Keep yourself informed about the global refugee crisis. Set up a Google Alert for the key word "refugee."
2. Pray together as a church or a small group — ask God to reveal to you what could you do as a group for refugees.
3. Tell a friend about this book and help us to increase awareness of the plight of refugees.

Reflections

_____

_____

_____

_____

_____

_____

_____

_____

_____

_____

_____

_____

_____

_____

_____

_____

_____

31.

The Calling

"The King will reply, 'I tell you the truth, whatever you did for one of the least of these brothers of mine, you did for me.'"

Matthew 25:40

At a certain point, I just felt, you know, God is not looking for alms, God is looking for action.

Bono

Nikos

Many have asked me why anyone would choose to go and work with refugees. And I answer: "Because I could not do otherwise." Either I had to stop praying to God to send more workers to minister in the Muslim countries, or I had to get involved personally with the thousands of Muslim refugees that God has brought into my country. When my wife and I decided, after a lot of prayer, to leave my job and join the Helping Hands ministry we didn't know what God was going to do. From the very beginning we learned that where God guides He provides.

Before joining the ministry full-time, I was serving the refugees as a volunteer. From that time, God has shown me that He knows how to provide, like that second Monday morning of January 2000, when I received a call at my work, from the teammate who was responsible for the shower ministry. He told me that we would not do the showers that day, because there were no towels. Without thinking at all, I said to him to stay where he is and to turn on the electrical water heater. I went home and I picked up all of the towels I could find, and ran to the Athens Refugee Center.

Then, one of our employees came to my office and said that because he is going on vacation and will miss my birthday, he decided to give me an early present. He gave me three large bags. When I opened them I started to cry. There were three full sets of new towels plus a bathrobe. At first he was confused. He thought I was offended by his present. I told him about the shower ministry, and he understood.

During one of our visits to the USA, while preaching at the Greek Evangelical Church of Pasadena in California, I showed a three-minute video about the Helping Hands ministry among the refugees in Athens. At the end of the service, three young men came to me, speaking in fluent Greek, and asked if I remembered them. Then they asked me to play the video again. When I did they pointed to their faces eating in the dining room of our center. They became Christians at Helping Hands and when they moved to Pasadena, they chose to join a Greek Church because, while in Greece, they learned Greek and could communicate better in Greek than in English.

One time an embassy official from an EU country came to my small office at Helping Hands. A four-member Iranian refugee family, who had become Christians at Helping Hands, went to his country and applied for asylum. Their embassy in Greece was investigating their claim. They wanted to know if their papers were legitimate or fake. I looked at the file the official presented me, while he asked me if I thought they were truly born again. I told him that he chose the right words, because if this family were not Christians, neither was I. As he was leaving, he turned around and said, "You know, they must be true Christians. In my country we move refugees from one camp to another. Wherever this family goes, they make the others Christians."

I have seen also how God uses the Helping Hands ministry to encourage other churches in Greece, in the USA and Canada to start similar ministries for refugees and the homeless. Part of my passion is to visit churches and share the miracles that God is doing among the refugees in Athens. As a result of these visits, a church in Arizona added to their new church building a shower and a clothing ministry for the homeless in their city.

The first new believers from their new ministry were from among the homeless. Two churches in Greece were encouraged by our ministry to start language classes to the children of immigrants, teaching them their mother language and in this way sharing with them and their parents about God's love.

So, if you ask me again why anyone would choose to work with refugees, I would have to say because it is a very powerful and effective way to reach out to the Muslim nations. Many refugees who accept Jesus in Greece move on to other parts of the world and spread the Gospel among their communities in their new homes. Some go back to their own countries, speaking about the Gospel of Salvation through Jesus Christ, delivering the message to places where foreigners wouldn't be able. While serving God by serving the refugees, I have seen the power of God in action. I have seen former Muslims declaring publicly their faith in Jesus as they were being baptized. I have seen the reproduction of the New Testament pattern of spreading the Gospel among their own people wherever they were going. I have also seen His protective power when one afternoon Scott and I were attacked by a mentally ill refugee. God was there and we left with only a small cut on Scott's underarm.

God is here every day and He leads us as we rely on His provision. I don't feel that by joining the ministry I missed out on anything. I feel richer than ever before by following the Lord in this ministry, and I have the unique opportunity to get to know God in ways I have not known Him ever before. Don't miss out on this great opportunity to reach out to refugees now, because I believe that we will be accountable to God and to history for this amazing opportunity to help change our world.

· ·

Rear-view Mirror

**Recent excerpts from ministry updates by
Helping Hands staff members.**

There is much to praise God for and intercede about these days from the ministry in Athens.

Here are a few examples: "I'm excited. God is changing lives here in Athens. We are already planning ten baptisms in the next few weeks. God is drawing people to Himself through Christ Jesus. That alone is exciting. But what really gets my heart pumping is how God is doing this: God is using refugees to reach refugees. Iranians reaching Iranians with the Gospel. Afghans leading Afghans to faith. Arabs sharing Christ with other Arabs. Please, join us in praising God for His work here."

"Our team mate Nader was sharing that recently an Iranian friend who lives in England was visiting and was telling about a man who is very influential in the Iranian church there. Nader thought he sounded familiar so Amir showed him a picture. Nader excitedly said, "I know this guy; I baptized him here in Athens!" We know of several fellowships in other countries headed up by believers who came to faith here at Helping Hands. Recently, we are also seeing more and more refugees sharing their faith right here in Athens.

"One new believer "M" is one of the women who came to our house for the first women's tea we had here. She accepted the Lord and since then she can be seen almost any time we are gathered, sitting at a table surrounded by women with her Farsi Bible open. Her husband is a new believer as well. Please pray for their spiritual growth and also that they can find work as they are struggling financially."

"In one of our last updates I shared about "N", the woman who had accepted the Lord and was afraid to let anyone know because her husband had beaten her for bringing home a Bible. God is doing amazing things. Her husband came to Persian Christian Fellowship and one of the refugee believers befriended him and began to share. He now attends regularly and can often be seen deep in conversation with Nader or other refugee believers. He is very close to accepting the Lord. Thank you for praying."
What do these testimonies reflect about the ministry of Helping Hands?

1. What, in your opinion, is the most exciting part of this mission?
2. To receive your own Helping Hands monthly newsletter, e-mail scott.mccracken@iteams.org Don't forget to mention this book.
3. Help us to spread the word. If you like this book, please tell your friends about it.

· ·

Reflections

_____

_____

_____

_____

_____

_____

_____

_____

_____

_____

_____

_____

_____

_____

_____

_____

_____

_____

_____

_____

Birds on a Wire

Kent Morley

Their country of birth was in such chaos that the main roads were freeways to death and every side street was an avenue of destruction. Only one narrow and perilous path provided an escape and so they embarked on this journey toward life. Refugees, foreigners, temporary dwellers in a land steeped in strangeness. Birds perched for a moment on a wire, searching the horizon for a safe spot to build a nest. This is reality for millions among us, those, just around the corner of the globe, just across the border. Jesus calls them our neighbors.

We are grateful to be your arms of caring and your message of hope to these battered brothers and sisters. Sons and daughters estranged from a Father who waits expectantly and watches intently to see who might be coming down the road toward home.

Admittedly we are all grateful that their plight is not ours. Yet, their vagrant condition ought to be a picture of our own spiritual standing and practice in whatever culture we reside. Peter, remembering the words that Jesus spoke to him: "you do not belong to this world, but I have chosen you out of the world", reminds us that we also are aliens and strangers in our own world. We are the foreign nomads in our familiar neighborhoods – strangers just passing through. Nesting for a season, precariously perched, watching the horizon, destined to fly home.

Perhaps the analogy ends here. The goal of most refugees is to find a place where they can feel at home. To find a place to blend in and have a normal life like those around them. To perhaps one day become citizens, to belong, to feel at home. Whereas, scripture reminds us pointedly and often that entangling ourselves in the ways of the world mandates untangling ourselves from our Father's embrace. "Friendship with the world is hostility toward God." In order to cozy up to the world we must distance ourselves from God. Our goal should never be to feel at home in a place where the things that God calls worthless are valued as priceless.

As those called out, let us come out, move out, and let us embrace our refugee status. Our refuge is not a where but, a whom. We are not in pursuit of a flag but, a cross. We are wanderers. Not hopeless wanderers but, wanderers whose hope is secure. Not homeless wanderers but, wanderers whose homes are being prepared. So pack lightly, too much stuff is just going to weigh you down on this journey down the refugee highway.

Perch lightly, always ready to fly.

Biblical Appendix

(Scriptural Support)

· ·

"The community is to have the same rules for you and for THE ALIEN living among you; this is a lasting ordinance for the generations to come. You and THE ALIEN shall be the same before the LORD."
Numbers 15:15, NIV

"THE ALIEN living with you must be treated as one of your native-born. Love him as yourself, for you were aliens in Egypt. I am the LORD your God."
Leviticus 19:34, NIV

"For the LORD your God is the God of gods and the Lord of lords, the great, the mighty, and the awesome God who does not show partiality nor take a bribe. HE executes justice for the orphan and the widow, and SHOWS HIS LOVE FOR THE ALIEN by giving him food and clothing. So SHOW YOUR LOVE FOR THE ALIEN, for you were ALIENS in the land of Egypt." Deuteronomy 10:17-19, NASB

"Celebrate the Feast of Tabernacles for seven days after you have gathered the produce of your threshing floor and your winepress. Be joyful at your Feast—you, your sons and daughters, your menservants and maidservants, and the Levites, THE ALIENS, the fatherless, and the widows who live in your towns. For seven days celebrate the Feast to the LORD your God."
Deuteronomy 16:13-14, NIV

"When you have finished setting aside a tenth of all your produce in the third year, the year of the tithe, you shall give it to the Levite, THE ALIEN, the fatherless, and the widow, so that they may eat in your towns and be satisfied."
Deuteronomy 26:12, NIV

"Assemble the people, the men and the women and children and THE ALIEN who is in your town in order that they may hear and learn and fear the LORD your God, and be careful to observe all the words of this law. THEIR CHILDREN, who have not known, will hear and learn to fear the LORD your God as long as you live on the land which you are about to cross the Jordan to possess."
Deuteronomy 31:12-13, NASB

"Then the righteous will answer him, 'Lord, when did we see You hungry and feed You, or thirsty and give You something to drink? When did we see you A STRANGER and invite You in, or needing clothes and clothe You? And when did we see You sick, or in prison, and come to You?'"
Matthew 25:37-39, NIV

"Do not neglect to show hospitality to STRANGERS, for by this some have entertained angels without knowing it."
Hebrews 13:2, NASB